SALES LEADERSHIP AT THE SUMMIT

VISION, GROWTH, AND BUILDING HIGH-PERFORMING TEAMS

Ahmed Yahya

TABLE OF CONTENTS

INTRODUCTION

W hat does it take to be a great sales leader? Assuming you work in sales, you have likely pondered this question before. Perhaps you have even come up with some answers for it. Maybe you reasoned that the mark of a great sales leader is the obvious: high and consistent sales figures. Maybe you decided it was something entirely different, like being able to craft really sound sales strategies or put together high-performing sales teams. Whatever the case, none of these answers is right, at least not by itself. You see, a good sales leader is not just defined by one thing; it is a conglomeration of features and skills.

This makes sense when you think about it. After all, a great sales leader is not just a great salesperson. They are so much more. A sales leader is the person who sets the tone and aspirations of the entire sales team they oversee. They are the one who shepherds that sales team, create their sales playbook, and define their goals, sales processes, long-term vision, and even their entire culture. That is a significant undertaking, being a great sales leader demands a highly specialized skill set and deep expertise. An exceptional leader does not just build a high-performing sales team; they keep it motivated, energized, and consistently delivering results. They can draw out the very best in the people they lead and collaborate with.

At the same time, they are an expert strategist who can read and interpret the marketplace they are operating in, quickly identify trends and upcoming trends, and take advantage of them. They are flexible enough to alter and tweak their plans when the need calls for it, resilient enough to support their team and company through times of change and turbulence, and innovative enough to open new paths for their business. They are also someone who can acquire new customers for their brand and inspire brand loyalty among them, turning them into long-term, if not life-long, customers and brand ambassadors.

Whichever way you see it, this is no small feat. The real question is not what makes a great sales leader, it is how you can become one. To be clear, you do not have to be a sales manager to become a great sales leader. The skills and knowledge that make a sales leader great do not come automatically with the position. Instead, they are cultivated over time and with diligence and care. No matter where they are in the corporate hierarchy, these are skills that anyone can learn and use. They are, in fact, skills that will make them shine among their peers, letting them distinguish themselves as the leaders they have the potential to be. By cultivating these skills, someone in a sales team can rapidly gain a reputation and success, propelling them to the leadership position they deserve. Similarly, a sales leader can cultivate and work on these skills to go from a competent or good leader to an exceptional one over time.

All of this, however, will take work and some dedication. No one can become an expert in their field overnight. Honing one's skills takes effort, and doing so is essential for sales leaders to be effective in their jobs and foster a positive work culture. Without refining their skills, they can neither develop nor execute robust sales strategies. Crafting meticulous action plans or coming up with goal-oriented approaches aligned with business objectives—two things a sales leader has to do if they are to succeed in their chosen line of work—will not be a possibility.

Sales leaders have a wide array of responsibilities to take care of. They must elevate their sales outcomes. They must understand their business's key performance indicators (KPIs) while conducting effective performance reviews. They must motivate their teams and address underperformance, if necessary. They must increase the efficiency and productivity of their teams by optimizing their business's sales processes, leveraging cutting-edge technologies, and harnessing data-driven insights to use for all future endeavors. They must always adopt a customer-first mentality while focusing on employing consultative selling techniques, building new, beneficial relationships, and delivering value-aligned solutions to their clients.

As if all that were not enough, great sales leaders must always remain agile and adapt to emerging market trends, changing customer needs, and new technological developments to stay current, relevant, and in demand in the market. Meanwhile, they must adopt a culture of continual learning by providing ongoing training and development opportunities to their team members to stay ahead in their business. Finally, they must embrace ethical standards and business practices, prioritizing integrity and transparency, particularly in sales transactions, to cultivate trust among their clients, shareholders, and other stakeholders. This practice fosters long-term loyalty.

So, what skills does a great sales leader need to possess and hone to be able to do all this, and how can you cultivate them? This is the very subject matter of this book: *The Strategic Sales Leader: Architecting Vision, Driving Growth.*

Now that you have picked up this book and started turning the pages, you are about to explore in depth what I have learned over a lifetime in sales leadership. These are not just theories, they are lessons earned through experience. Over the years, I have built my career across sales management, general management, consulting, coaching, and mentoring. I have seen what works, what fails, and what transforms good teams into great ones.

It all started with my role as a Sales Analyst at General Motors, where I learned the fundamentals of strategy and performance. I later became a Sales Trainer for GM dealers in Saudi Arabia, sharpening my skills in team development and communication. Eventually, I took on a bold new challenge, leading the sales team of a startup dealership. Under my sales leadership, that dealership quickly rose to the top, selling thousands of vehicles in just a few years and establishing the dealership as one of the leading automotive brands in the country.

What you will find in this book is a collection of lessons, hard-earned, battle-tested, and ready to serve any sales leader aiming to make a real impact.

My goal in writing this book is to share the lessons and experiences with those working in these various roles so that they can take advantage of what I have learned more quickly and easily than I did. It is to provide them with a guide of sorts in their sales journey, no matter where they might be in their career. This book, though, is more than just a guide. It would be more accurate to say that it is a mentor, a trusted resource that equips you, the reader, with the tools you need to navigate the complex landscape of sales management.

With this mentor by your side, or, more accurately, in your hands, you now possess all you need to become the best sales leader you can be. You have everything you need to hone the skills to achieve the greatness you aspire to. All you need to do is turn the page to access and learn how to use them.

CHAPTER 1

UNDERSTANDING SALES MANAGEMENT FUNDAMENTALS

———————◆———————

Great salespeople are relationship builders who provide value and help their customers win.

–Jeffrey Gitomer

Before we can dive into the various skills you need to adopt and hone to become the great sales leader within you, we first need to grasp what a sales leader is and what they do. We need to ensure that we properly understand sales management fundamentals. If you are wondering why that is the case, imagine that you are building a house. You have a fantastic design on your hands, and you cannot wait to get started. Before you can build that house, you need to lay down a strong, stable foundation for it. If you do not, that house will ultimately collapse, no matter how pretty. Obviously, in this metaphor, your "house" represents your efforts and strategy as a sales leader or even a sales manager, which means that knowing and understanding your fundamentals differentiates between a winning strategy and a successful career and a disastrous outcome.

A Sales Leader? What Is That?

Many people confuse "sales leaders" with "sales managers" and vice versa. This is an easy mistake, seeing as managers are in leadership positions. However, this does not change the fact that sales leaders and managers have distinct roles. A sales leader develops entire sales strategies for their sales team (Indeed Editorial Team, 2023b). They are the individuals who train the managers who will oversee their businesses' sales teams. Sales managers are a rung below sales leaders in the corporate hierarchy. They are the individuals who are the heads of their own sales teams, and they are in charge of coaching and training those teams based on what they have learned from their sales leaders.

The scope of a sales leader's responsibilities is very different from that of a sales manager's. A sales leader, for instance, uses data-driven insights to set long-term goals for the sales department. Meanwhile, sales managers oversee their specific sales teams to ensure those goals are ultimately met. Leaders, in essence, are the individuals who decide on the vision, strategy, goals, and processes of sales teams. On the other hand, managers are the individuals who work to execute those strategies and goals, manage those processes, and ensure that the decided-on vision is achieved. In layperson's terms, sales leaders are the decision-makers, while managers are the ones who ensure those decisions are acted on and that their intended goals are achieved.

While our book focuses on the skills you need to adopt and hone to become a great sales leader, it does not mean that individuals who are not sales leaders cannot still learn from this book. They can and should, especially if they want to become sales leaders later. The skills that make a great sales leader are not only useful for sales managers but also for salespeople in various aspects of their jobs. Moreover, these skills will also help them become sales leaders later on, if they desire, and tackle the responsibilities that come with this position effectively.

A sales leader has a wide array of responsibilities to take care of. For one, they must create a sales strategy that is best and most appropriate for the business or company that they are a part of (Kumar, 2022). This sales strategy must be one that will prove motivating for their business's sales teams, since they will be using it. It also must play into those teams' strengths. For another, sales leaders must consistently meet the revenue and sales goals set for their business or company. At the same time, they must train their sales managers and teams in the sales strategy they have developed and the various methods and tactics that go with it. Then, they must write current reports on sales figures, present them to upper management, and use the data they have obtained from these figures to understand what is working in their strategy and what is not working. Using that information, they must adjust their strategy where necessary and train their managers and teams on the changes they are implementing.

Sales leaders also must set realistic quotes and expectations for their sales team and its various members. They must develop new, appropriate methods for reaching new customers and maintaining the loyalty of existing ones, which means they must be innovative at times. They must continually conduct lead conversations through various channels, identify and develop ways to cross-sell and upsell to existing customers, and create new accounts while managing existing ones.

As you can see, sales managers have their work cut out for them. Sales managers must do all this and do it well. Otherwise, their sales teams will be left directionless and in chaos. Sales leaders are crucial to a brand to prevent this from happening, and there are several reasons why this is the case. One is that sales leaders help manage and maintain a sales team's focus, energy, and motivation, as you will see in later chapters (*Importance of a Sales Manager*, 2012). Another is that they enable sales teams to develop healthy, long-term, and sustainable internal decision-making processes and habits that thus lead to sustainable sales-business practices. Sales leaders are also vital for brands because they help grow the businesses that they are a part of. They also provide their company or organization with a sound and reliable leadership structure and a good coaching or training system. Best of all, they set clear expectations for everyone in the sales department, from managers down to employees, leaving little to no room for confusion or misunderstandings and elevating everyone's performance levels. As an interesting side effect, they cultivate an environment of greater accountability, attracting more talent to that brand's sales department and company. This has the additional benefit of increasing employee retention—a goal pursued by all companies.

The Sales Ecosystem

A sales leader's ability to do all this is contingent on their ability to understand the sales ecosystem they are a part of. The sales ecosystem comprises the sales process, the stakeholders involved in it, and how their sales teams work and are structured. Let us tackle that sentence piece by piece for a minute. For example, what exactly is a "sales process?" Well, the sales process is the method that you, as a sales leader, and the business that you are a part of, follow to sell a product or service to others. In a way, building a sales process is a bit like building a new relationship. First, you and your customer get to know each other (Gargaro, 2023). At this stage, you understand what your customer wants, needs, and likes. Then, you come to grasp what their goals are. Based on that information, you determine whether the customer is a good match for your business and the product or service you're offering them. If they are, you keep the conversation moving forward. If they are not, you know when to call in your chips and move on to the next conversation with the next potential customer.

A sales leader or manager must build a sound sales process to help them identify the main challenges they'll face in the market before they ever face them. Thus, it enables them to develop appropriate solutions to those problems. A good sales process also enables sales managers or leaders to optimize and enhance their team members' performance levels while facilitating the scalability of those teams over time. Having such a sales process in place further enables them to take stock of all the available resources, identify which resources are being wasted and why, and then eliminate activities and initiatives that prove wasteful. This frees up a great deal of resources, time, effort, and energy for all involved in the sales process. Teams, managers, and leaders can now focus on initiatives that yield a better investment return and, therefore, don't waste any resources.

Now that you know what a sales process is and why it's important, let's look at the stakeholders. "Stakeholder" is a catch-all term for all the individuals and groups affected by the decisions a company's sales team makes. Hence, the term encompasses customers, shareholders, investors, partners, consultants, and employees. Among these different stakeholders, the ones that sales leaders focus mainly, though not exclusively, on are customers. This is because a brand or company cannot exist if it doesn't have any customers, which is why sound sales processes always begin with a sales leader making an effort to identify and understand their customers, a subject matter you'll be learning a great deal about in Chapter 3.

It's worth noting that there are several methods a sales leader can use to identify and understand their customers. Two of the most popular methods among renowned sales leaders are customer stakeholder mapping and building an **ideal customer profile** (ICP). The first of these methods, customer stakeholder mapping, is a process that works well for businesses with an existing customer base. A sales leader in such a business can begin the process by defining the goals and interests of their customers. By doing so, they can identify the right prospective customers. They can then tailor their offer to suit those customers specifically. That way, when they're presenting their offer, they will be able to make sure that it's according to their customers' needs, wants, and interests, making said offer much more appealing (Bray, 2023).

Once a sales leader has identified their customers' goals and interests, they can divide them into various groups, depending on their roles, attitudes, general influence, and budget, as part of the customer stakeholder mapping process. That way, they can tailor their offer according to their customers. Once this is done, they can finally move on to mapping stakeholder relationships, meaning their internal sales team's relationship with their external stakeholders, specifically their customers. They can focus on strengthening and nurturing the relationship between these two entities, thereby fortifying the sales process and winning lifelong, loyal customers.

Alternatively, a sales leader can use the ICP method to understand their customers. ICP starts with a sales leader trying to understand their customers by building a profile of what their ideal customer looks like, a concept explored in more detail in the coming chapters. Such a profile will make it possible for them to quickly identify the right prospect to contact and then reach out to them. Like the mapping method, ICP's profile building requires understanding the ideal customer's needs and wants, as well as their roles, attitudes, general influence, and budget (Van Rensburg, 2022). It includes basic demographic information about them, like their gender and age. The ICP essentially uses real, concrete data from real customers to create a fictional generalization of a brand's ideal customer. This ideal customer is someone who can add value to a company or brand, and that brand could provide value in the form of a return on investment by meeting a need or in some other way.

Having identified and understood their customers, the sales leader's next step in the sales process is to contact prospective customers, meaning the individuals they intend to target. For this, the sales leader needs to identify the best possible "leads" that fit the profile they created. As they do so, they can create a list of potential candidates, like client companies, that their sales team can contact in due course. They narrow this list by researching those individuals or organizations. They can then try to determine whether these individuals or organizations need the product or service that their brand is offering, have the budget to purchase it, are authorized to make the purchase, and if the timing is right for them to do so.

This sales process is usually followed up by sales leaders qualifying their prospects. Qualifying prospects is a fancy way of saying that sales leaders have to see whether the prospects they have found can be converted into long-term, if not life-long, customers. Unlike previous steps, it involves contacting the prospects that have been identified. Sales leaders have to figure out the best way to contact the prospects they have identified because a method that works for one individual or organization may not work for another. For example, older people prefer phone calls to emails and text messages. Younger generations, like millennials, on the other hand, prefer doing things via email and text (Alton, 2017). So, if you contact a prospective millennial customer via email instead of calling them, your chances of making a successful sale will be much higher. Your chances of success will similarly rise if you go into a sales conversation fully prepared. This means learning more about your prospects in conversation, which can only be done by talking with them. This will help you gain clarity on a variety of factors and help you better determine whether that prospect is a good fit or not.

If a sales leader can qualify, the sales process will move on to nurturing the relationship they are building. Suppose they are unable to qualify a prospect. In that case, the sales process for that individual or organization will end, and the sales leader will move on to the next prospect on this list. Assuming they have been able to qualify a prospect, their next step will be to make their offer officially, and this is when they will see whether their efforts to court their prospects have worked (Gargaro, 2023). At this stage, some resistance or objections are to be expected, and sales leaders anticipate them. They understand how to present their perspective and demonstrate why their solution is the right choice. Familiar with common objections, they are prepared to counter them with confidence. Once addressed, they can move to close the deal, bringing the sales process for that customer to a successful conclusion.

A Brief History Of Sales Management

When you take it all in like this, the sales process may seem like rather obvious information, but it is anything but. At least, it was for a time, given how long it took for sales processes to become standard procedures or for sales management to become an acknowledged, official field of its own, for that matter. The history of sales is a somewhat complicated one in several ways. Sales have been a part of human history for as long as money has existed. However, that does not mean it was regarded as a respected practice. It took years, even centuries, for working in sales to become a respectable endeavor.

Take the Roman Empire, for example. Did you know that the Roman word for salesperson means cheater? (Limaye & Pande, 2016) Did you know that this interpretation of sales and salespeople endured for centuries? Of course, the view that salespeople were cheaters started changing over time as the world became more international and connected. As trade with other nations and cultures increased, new trade routes opened, and thus, new sales opportunities arose. India, for instance, became a significant destination for traders in the Medieval Age. As trade routes like the Spice Road and, later, a wide variety of ocean routes opened up, traders started gaining a reputation as trustworthy, worldly, and cultural individuals. As part of their travels and business, they got acquainted with the beliefs and cultures of other countries, the countries with which they did business. Trade thus became as much a vehicle for exchanging new ideas and inventions with people worldwide as it was about sales (*Evolution of Sales Management*, 2022).

Sales were introduced to the United States later than to various European countries. The first real salespeople in the US were peddlers. Peddlers would go from town to town, village to village, to sell their goods. In the 19th century, they began using horse-driven wagons and carts to carry heavier goods to sell, such as weapons and furniture. Some peddlers eventually began settling down in villages. There, they opened the first-ever stores. One of the first examples of this was seen not in the United States but in India, among a trading caste known as Baniyas. The idea, however, rapidly spread around the world. Wholesalers started cropping up in various countries. Of course, store owners need to get the word out about their stores to attract customers and make sales now. This need gave rise to a new kind of advertising campaign: drummers. Store owners and wholesalers started sending drummers to train stations to draw customers to their stores and beat out their competitors. Over time, this became standard practice. You can imagine how loud and, therefore, headache-inducing a standard practice it must have been.

Luckily, this sales practice would go out of fashion. In time, it would be replaced by other sales practices as the sales landscape itself changed. These changes were initially small and gradual, at least until the Industrial Revolution. The beginning of the Industrial Revolution, the mid-18th century, was a turning point for the sales industry. Around this time, salespeople's numbers doubled, then tripled on a global scale, and continued to increase over time. Such was the backdrop of the sales industry when a man called John Henry Patterson came onto the scene. At the time, Patterson ran the National Cash Registry. Looking for a way to optimize the sales process, he turned his attention to his best salespeople. He then asked them to demonstrate and teach their best techniques to their peers. His approach worked like a charm. Sales figures suddenly increased, making his entire sales team infinitely more effective.

Having observed this, Patterson made an interesting decision. He decided to share what he had learned and began sharing with others rather than keeping it to himself. To that end, he had his best salespeople write down their techniques. He then had them printed and distributed as a sales primer, which he naturally sold to others. Thus,

Patterson became the father of modern sales management. Of course, his efforts did not stop there. Patterson went on to do far more to earn his new reputation. For instance, he started giving his salespeople exclusive territories to work in and meeting quotas. To his delight, he observed that this made everyone more efficient and productive. Patterson also started holding regular sales meetings. In time, these meetings became venues for socialization and training. They did not just increase people's productivity but also their motivation to work by making them feel more connected to others and the company they were a part of. Patterson also took mentorship quite seriously, believing it to be an important part of sales management. This is why he trained Thomas J. Watson, who would later form IBM.

There is no denying that Patterson made tremendous contributions to sales management. However, the field has evolved beyond his vision since its inception. It grew beyond what Patterson had envisioned and took on a life of its own. As it did, people's perceptions of salespeople changed even further. In the past, most considered salespeople to be order takers. Today, salespeople are seen as strategists and consultants whose primary focus and priority is addressing the problems and needs of their customers and prospective customers. This is why, over the years, sales focus has turned from getting new customers to retaining existing customers, though new customers are still important. In other words, sales leaders started focusing more on customer loyalty, ensuring continued, steady sales for years.

CHAPTER 2

BUILDING AND LEADING HIGH-PERFORMANCE SALES TEAMS

Pretend that every single person you meet has a sign around his or her neck that says, 'Make me feel important.' Not only will you succeed in sales, you will succeed in life.

–Mary Kay Ash

You might think a sales leader's job starts with strategizing. You would be wrong. Strategizing is undoubtedly a significant part of a sales leader's job. It's, in fact, part of their very job description. However, there is one thing that a sales leader needs to consider before they can even begin thinking about their sales strategy: their team. The first thing a sales leader needs to do is put together a high-performance sales team capable of flawlessly executing the strategy they will develop. Think of this team as a sales leader's Avengers. Said leader can come up with the best strategy humanly possible. However, that strategy will never be executed successfully as they are not able to assemble the Avengers, Iron Man, Captain America, and more. So, how does one put together such a team? How can you find the perfect superheroes, so to speak, for your sales team? How can you make sure that the team works well and effectively together? How can you lead that team in a way that inspires its members to do their best and utmost for the brand they represent and the company they are a part of? Let us find out.

Recruiting Sales Talent

A sales leader's strategy is only as good as the sales teams they put together. The people making up your sales team are the ones who will be executing, maybe even contributing to your strategy, after all. Hence, you want those teams to comprise the most talented, motivated, and hard-working people possible. You want those team members to work harmoniously together. You want them to be dedicated to their work and have the necessary skills to execute their responsibilities well.

As a rule, you want to recruit the best talent for your sales team, that is only natural. Equally important, however, is ensuring you hire individuals whose skills, temperament, and strengths align with the specific roles they will fill and the responsibilities they will be expected to carry out. Say that you are the sales leader of a meditation app, for instance. You are looking to fill a position in one of your sales teams, and there seem to be two excellent candidates. You are caught between them. One of these candidates is deeply interested in meditation. They meditate daily and have been doing so for years. They practice yoga weekly, too, and are generally very into wellness culture. The other candidate has excellent credentials but is not interested in meditation. They find it somewhat irritating. They seem to think that meditation is an empty trend that will wither away in time. Which candidate, then, do you think is a better fit for the job?

The answer to that question is "the first one." This is an easy answer to figure out. After all, no matter how good and experienced your second candidate is, they will not be able to do a good job selling your meditation app, no matter how hard they try. If you were to hire them, you would be hiring someone who would not buy what they are selling.

This kind of inauthenticity is why salespeople were regarded as "cheats" back in ancient times. It is also something that customers and prospective customers can easily pick up on. Hiring a salesperson who does not believe in what they are selling is bad business practice and something to watch out for. So is hiring salespeople who do not like being and working in sales. The simple fact is that such an individual will not be as motivated to do their best work and be as productive as other salespeople, no matter how hard they try.

In essence, you need two things to hire the right salespeople for your sales team. First, you must find individuals who believe in the product or service they will be tasked with selling. Second, you will have to find people who enjoy their job. That way, you will be able to ensure that the sales team you form remains authentic, hard-working, motivated, and highly productive. However, these are not the only requirements for forming a high-performing sales team. There are others. There are various strategies you can adopt when hiring people for your sales teams. One such strategy is to plan what your perfect sales candidate looks like.

Here is the thing: Your definition of the "perfect sales candidate" is not going to be the same as someone else's. If you were the sales leader of a meditation app, then your definition of the ideal candidate would be very different from the definition of the sales leader that a pharmaceutical company would adopt, now, would it? Meanwhile, the ideal candidate's definition, according to that pharmaceutical candidate's sales leader, would differ significantly from that of a video game company that is putting out a new action-adventure role-playing game (RPG) on the market.

So, the first thing a sales leader must figure out is their

definition of the ideal sales candidate. To figure out the nswer to this question, you are going to have to ask yourself specific questions, such as

- What kind of experience level do I want my ideal sales candidate to have?
- What unique skills must my sales candidate have to be able to do their job well?
- What kind of educational background do I want my candidate to come from?
- What interests should my ideal sales candidate have in being able to sell the product or service my company offers?
- What value must they possess?
- What kind of work ethic should my candidate have?
- What kind of personality must my ideal salesperson have?

That last question might seem a little out of place at first glance, but it makes sense if you consider it. Whatever sales candidate a sales leader hires will ultimately be a part of one of their sales teams. It is important to choose those individuals who can work well with others and, thus, create a harmonious work environment for all instead of a toxic one. If you choose the right person with the right temperament, everyone will work well together. Thus, salespeople will be able to collaborate with one another, stay energized and motivated as they work, and maintain high performance levels. Hiring the wrong person with the wrong temperament, however, can lead to a sales team riddled with tension, conflict, and maybe even arguments. This will divert everyone's focus, causing their motivation and energy levels to decrease. Team members won't be able to collaborate effectively and easily. Their productivity and performance levels will, therefore, go down. If things go on in this fashion for long enough, employee turnover rates might even start climbing, which is never good.

A sales candidate's personality is not just important for their ability to work well with their sales team, but also for their ability to make sales. You see, a good salesperson has certain personality traits that make them very good at their job. To be more specific, they have four distinct personality traits that can make them the perfect salespeople, with a little bit of experience. These personality traits are:

- confidence
- resilience
- competitiveness
- persistence

To understand why these four traits are "musts" for good salespeople, we must look closely at them, starting with confidence. Imagine that you are looking to buy sunscreen. Your one requirement for the product you are going to buy is that it be free of harmful chemicals. You know of two stores that sell such sunscreen. You visit both locations and talk with one salesperson at each location. The first salesperson at the store you go to is a nervous, somewhat self-conscious fellow. They stammer through their explanation as to why their sunscreen is excellent. They cannot confidently back up their claims that this is the brand of sunscreen you want to buy. They answer your questions in a halting, hesitant manner. As a result, you leave the store unconvinced about the sunscreen they were trying to sell you.

You head to the second store next. There, the salesperson who greets you is very confident. They discuss the product they are trying to sell with enthusiasm and highlight its merits. They back up what they have to say with facts and testimonies. They answer your questions quickly, accurately, and without hesitation. You don't have any doubts left in your mind when you're done at the store. Now, which salesperson will you buy from: the first one or the second one?

This anecdote demonstrates why you want the salespeople you hire to be confident. However, you also want them to be resilient. You see, no matter how great a salesperson is, they will not be able to make a sale every single time they contact prospective customers. Throughout their career, they will hear the word "no" quite often. You want the salespeople you hire to be resilient because such individuals will not let the word "no" affect them. They will not let rejection diminish their motivation, enthusiasm, or confidence. Instead, they will be able to move on from it quickly and confidently tackle their next pitch, making the next sale. Thus, they will remain productive and successful, even on days when they feel like they get more "nos" than anything else.

Competitiveness is also a trait you are looking for in your salespeople because, simply put, the sales world is a competitive one. Businesses and brands compete against one another to hook the same customers. Salespeople compete against one another as they strive to be the best. A competitive salesperson can and will try their hardest to get the most sales and inspire customer loyalty as much as possible. They are always looking for new opportunities and will keep trying, regardless of any hurdles that come their way.

Finally, there is persistence. This is an important quality for salespeople because convincing a prospect to buy a product or service can take a while. It is a process. During this process, a salesperson will meet with questions, doubts, skepticism, resistance, and objections. The customer will ask them why they should choose the brand they are trying to sell. They will come up with excuses as to why they cannot choose this brand. They might even compare the brand the salesperson is trying to sell with others, asking what makes it different. A salesperson must tackle all these obstacles while building a relationship with the prospect. They will have to further the sales process, addressing the prospects' questions, doubts, concerns, and objectives until they are put to rest, and convincing them to buy. All that requires no small degree of persistence. Without it, the salesperson will give up midway through the process and potentially lose out on a lifelong customer.

So, you know what kind of personality the next salesperson you hire must have. You also know what your definition of the ideal sales candidate is. What is next? Well, you must put everything together in a job description. The job description you write and advertise must include all these different elements that you have figured out. This is the only way to ensure that the individuals who apply for the position you are advertising meet the ideal candidate criteria. True, the person who fits your definition of the ideal candidate might still apply for the position you are advertising, even if your job description does not feature all this information we have covered. However, the likelihood of you finding that person among the applications sent in decreases dramatically in this instance. After all, the vagueness of the job description will cause many who do not fit your definition of the ideal candidate to apply to your company. Finding the right candidate's application among this influx will be akin to finding a needle in a haystack, to use a well-worn cliché.

Once you've written your job description and read it

over a few times to ensure it contains all the information it needs, you can finally post it and let the world know your sales team has an opening. The general policy you want to adopt at this stage is to post your job description on various platforms, including job boards and networking sites like LinkedIn. You also want to get the word out through networking events and social media platforms, such as Twitter. Using social media platforms is a great way to ensure that your company remains on the radar of the candidates you want for your team. For instance, you can post content on social media sites that will appeal to potential candidates, even when you're not hiring. Such content will get potential candidates interested in your company. Thus, they'll be eager to apply when you advertise that you are looking to hire new salespeople. Doubling down on this strategy during the hiring process will also increase your chances of attracting the right candidate.

Once you get your job description, you will inevitably receive a score of applications. To find the perfect candidates for the open sales position, you will have to carefully screen the stack of CVs or resumes that have been sent your way. The first step of this process will be to find the candidates who best match the profile you created. Odds are, you will not find a candidate who fits your description to a tee. You will, however, be able to find plenty that get as close to your description as possible. The candidates you decide to interview and consider are the ones who make up that pool.

As you likely know, interviews are a vital part of the hiring process. You can learn a lot about a candidate through their cover letter and resume, of course, but you can learn much more about them in a face-to-face interview. The interview is where you assess your candidates' skills, experience, and motivations for wanting to join your sales team. It is where you evaluate them to see if they would be the best fit for your team and the position you have advertised. It is a data-gathering operation, so to speak, where you get a feel for each candidate and assess whether they would make a good fit for your sales teams. Sometimes, candidates prove very different from what their resumes suggest. Other times, you find that a candidate who is perfect on paper would create a lot of discord and tension among your sales team, which means that they are far from the ideal candidate you thought they were. Furthermore, you will be able to compare the skills, personalities, and experiences of two candidates you are caught between more accurately after interviewing them.

Of course, making such determinations will necessitate asking the right questions. The right questions to ask the candidates you are considering go beyond their education, skills, and professional experience. They also have to do with their selling styles, ability to manage expectations, and closing skills. Hence, you want to prepare a broad range of questions to help you assess these factors. As you are conducting an interview, one important rule you must remember is that if someone looks too good to be true, it is likely because they are. This is why you must do your due diligence after your interviews and call your clients' references. Doing so can spare you a lot of trouble, tension, and grief later.

Another thing you must remember about interviews is that first impressions matter. This goes both for the candidates you're seeing and for you, as the representative of the sales department and the brand you are a part of. You must endeavor to make a good first impression on the candidates you are interviewing. Otherwise, your ideal candidate might decline to work with you, which will be an unfortunate loss of talent for your sales department. One way to ensure you make a good first impression in interviews is to reflect on the quality of the product or service your sales department offers before the interview begins. Doing so will help you instill the sense that the candidate will be selling a quality product they can be proud of. It can also help you infuse them with a sense of purpose once they become a part of one of your sales teams.

Another way to make a good first impression is to showcase your success in the office where you are interviewing. Visual aids, like any certificates or awards you may have on display, can help with this. You can give your candidates a tour of the office, thus demonstrating the office environment to them and what their prospective co-workers are like. Finally, you can cement the first impression you give by taking care of your appearance and the interview space. Interviewing someone in a neat, organized space will give a very different impression than in a space riddled with rubbish and in disarray.

Team Dynamics

It goes without saying that finding the right candidates for your sales teams is just the start. At the end of the day, the candidate you decide on will be part of the team that you are creating. You want the various individuals making up that team to work well together. You want them to create an energetic, high-performing, highly motivated team. To that end, you must create a positive, nurturing environment where your team members can flourish and thrive. That means you must create a positive work culture and environment for all. This is important because studies show that creating such a work environment increases employee productivity by 12% and increases workplace profitability by 21% (Beheshti, 2019).

Your first order of business here is to decide what kind of positive work culture you want to create for your sales teams. The truth is that there are multiple different work cultures you can choose from, as you will see momentarily. One is not essentially better than the other. So, the trick here is not necessarily choosing the "best" work culture. Instead, it is choosing the "best one for you." Choosing the right work culture for your workplace requires defining your company's or organization's primary purpose. That way, you will be able to clearly and effectively communicate that purpose to others, like your team members. Having understood and connected with this higher purpose, your team members will be able to grasp the impact their work will ultimately have on others. They will be able to see how meaningful that work is. This will ultimately make them more committed, interested, and motivated to work.

This leads to a pivotal question: how do you discover your business's higher purpose? Begin by asking yourself, beyond profits, beyond products, what are we here to accomplish, and why does it matter? A technology company might strive to simplify life for millions. Another might aim to build a more sustainable world. The purpose is the heartbeat of the business, and until you find it, everything else is just motion without meaning. Perhaps they are trying to improve people's health in some way. Perhaps they are trying to do something entirely different. Whatever the case, once you have answered this question, you can turn your attention to your sales teams. You can ask yourself who among them exemplifies the values and purpose that your business is about. Who among them exemplifies the change and culture your brand is trying to create?

The individuals you identify by asking these questions

can be considered your culture champions. A good sales leader does not just stop identifying who their culture champions are. They take their efforts further and actively and openly acknowledge their contributions and successes. Do not get me wrong, it is important to acknowledge all your salespeople's achievements. However, doing so is especially important for your culture champions because it will provide them with opportunities to showcase the experiences and values they embody. It will allow them to demonstrate the qualities you want your sales teams to have, encouraging others to mirror and emulate their behavior. Hence, it is vital to reward employees whose behaviors align with the company's values and goals. This will give everyone an incentive to keep up the good work.

Praise and rewards are important but so is receiving honest feedback from your sales team members. Clear and open communication typically characterizes a positive work environment and culture. A lack of communication can be disastrous for a workplace. It can give rise to confusion and misunderstandings, generate unnecessary conflict and tension, and hinder people's ability to perform their jobs effectively. Open communication is not just about giving instructions, praise, and feedback to your sales team members. It is equally about receiving honest feedback from them because communication is a two-way street.

In a workplace where employees can give feedback to their managers and leaders, miscommunication issues can be resolved quickly. It is one where problems can be identified and relayed to upper management strata before they become major issues, allowing them to be resolved rapidly and efficiently. It is a setting where sales team members can unhesitatingly share new, innovative ideas with their leaders and, in the process, establish ways that can significantly benefit the company and its sales teams.

With all this in mind, it is easy to see that establishing a positive work culture requires placing special importance on good, clear communication. Of course, this is not the only thing sales leaders need to do to establish the kind of work culture they want. They must do a couple of other things, like setting rules, policies, and guidelines that prioritize their team members' well-being, safety, and happiness. This is important because employees who are healthy and happy at the workplace are inevitably more motivated, energized, and productive.

Focusing on the happiness of your team members is as effective a way of establishing a positive work culture as pursuing a policy of continued learning and development for your sales teams. Sales leaders must provide their team members with ample opportunities to learn and develop new skills, expand their knowledge, and gain new experiences. In other words, they must invest actively in their team members' development.

You can take a couple of additional measures to establish a positive work culture. One is to set clear, realistic objectives to guide team members' performance. Setting such goals and objectives for sales team members can increase their efficiency and productivity significantly. It can also significantly eliminate workplace confusion, making everyone more effective in their roles. Meanwhile, ensuring that all employees understand the company's short- and long-term goals, regardless of their position in the corporate hierarchy, can increase their alignment with the company's overall purpose, trajectory, and values. It can increase their sense of belonging, helping them to re-double their efforts as members of their sales teams. Thus, under your leadership, sales team members can shine and make it possible for the product or service they are selling to outshine all others in the market.

Leadership Skills

There is one word in that previous sentence that may have caught your attention for a moment: leadership. Sales leaders are precisely what their titles say they are: leaders. That means they need to possess specific leadership skills, which can unite the teams they manage and help each member make those teams shine as brightly as possible.

There is a wide variety of leadership skills one might possess. However, some are more essential to sales leaders than others due to their role. Overall, there are nine leadership skills an effective sales leader needs to have. These are:

- the ability to lead by example
- coaching skills
- the ability to communicate expectations clearly
- analytical and critical thinking abilities
- organizational skills
- sales planning
- delegation
- active listening
- problem solving

To start with, the ability to lead by example is a vital skill for sales leaders because it allows them to demonstrate the techniques, methods, and skills they want their team members to use. As you will recall, a sales leader's job is to train the sales managers and teams working under them. Teaching is an art, one that can come in a variety of styles. Leading by example is a teaching style in and of itself, and it is a particularly effective one. This is because when you lead by example, you remind your trainees what you want them to do and how you want them to do it with your actions. You do so every day, and in the process, you get to drive your lessons home. You inspire your trainees to model and emulate your behavior, making things much easier for all involved.

When considered in that light, the ability to lead by example is intimately connected to coaching skills, another asset that sales leaders need to possess. Coaching skills are part and parcel of sales leaders' ability to train their sales teams. So, what exactly do they entail? Coaching skills entail building and delivering effective training programs that heighten sales team members' performance and potential. These skills include identifying areas of improvement for individual members and teams and creating training programs and materials that all members can easily understand, digest, and learn from. Coaching skills even include providing team members with continued support and feedback. This way, team members can keep improving themselves and their performance. They can pick up new skills along the way or hone existing ones, the way one would sharpen a blade. These new or developing skills can come in handy when team members face unexpected challenges. For example, if a sales team member has picked up some copyediting skills, they might think of a way to improve the pitch they have to work with. This, in turn, could help them land more accounts and appeal to more people.

Strong coaching skills signal to your team that they can, and should, come to you when they are struggling, need support, or have identified a problem. At the heart of great coaching lies great communication. While communication matters in every setting, it is critical in sales, especially when conveying goals, expectations, and priorities to your team.

Many workplace delays, setbacks, and mistakes stem from unclear instructions or poorly communicated objectives.

In sales, that lack of clarity can have serious consequences, from losing a key account to creating unnecessary delays, tension, and confusion. Clear, consistent communication is not just a nice-to-have; it is the foundation for a high-performing sales team. Sales leaders must always maintain open communication with their team. The most effective approach is to keep messages, whether spoken or written, concise, clear, and straightforward. That is just one measure, though. There are additional measures to ensure clear communication between you and your sales teams. One is to hold yourself accountable for your words. This way, you can take responsibility for mistakes, such as miscommunication, and quickly fix them. You can inspire the members of your sales teams to do the same, thereby minimizing any problems that can arise from communication issues in the process.

Sales leaders can use various ways to communicate with their team members. There are emails, phone calls, Slack messages, and more. Sometimes, you have no choice but to use one of these methods. However, whenever possible, you should opt to communicate face-to-face with your sales team members. That is another way to ensure you are communicating with team members openly and clearly, especially since you can tell whether they have correctly understood something you have said to them from their expression in most cases.

Face-to-face communication will also afford the conversation a level of intimacy. It would be easier for a team member to come to you about a problem they have observed in person than to email you. If a problem is sensitive, you typically want to discuss it face-to-face rather than shoot an email about it. That way, you can avoid misunderstandings and miscommunications and ensure everyone properly understands the problem's urgency.

One final way to sharpen your communication skills is to follow up face-to-face conversations with written confirmation. For example, if you have assigned a sales team member a new project, send a follow-up email summarizing the key points and agreements from your discussion. While you are at it, always be sure that you keep your emotions in check when talking to your sales team. Consider this: When would you feel more comfortable approaching your sales leader with a problem, when you know they will react with anger and frustration, or when you know they will stay calm, keep their composure, and focus on finding a solution?

Communication skills are important for sales leaders, as you have seen. So are analytical and critical thinking skills. Analytical and critical thinking skills are monumental parts of a sales leader's life. This is because these skills allow them to thoroughly analyze any challenges, quickly identify their root causes, and efficiently solve them by addressing those root causes (Marr, 2022). They give sales leaders the ability to find new opportunities for sales growth by analyzing new market trends, rapidly identifying patterns they can use, and connecting different pieces of information. This allows them to make more informed decisions quickly, which can be vital in a business setting.

A sales leader can do a couple of things to develop their critical thinking and analytical skills, of course. One is to push yourself to regard any new information cautiously. Say that you have just gotten some new sales data for a new version of a product your company has put on the market. You want to make sure you are making the proper inferences from this data. That entails making sure you have the whole picture. So, you ask yourself whether the data at hand is complete. You ask whether it is up to date. You even ask whose, or which demographic's, information is missing.

Another way to hone your analytical and critical thinking skills is to evaluate the source of your information and consider multiple perspectives. Additionally, you must ask as many questions as possible and seek out extra information where needed. That way, you can train your mind to think more critically about facts, data, and insights whenever they are presented to you, fostering the capability to make better, more well-rounded decisions.

One of the most important skills a sales leader can possess is organizational skills. Organizational skills can be described as a sales leader's ability to prioritize, set goals, and achieve their desired ends while managing their time well. Such skills can be invaluable when sales leaders have multiple accounts and deadlines to manage. There are many organizational methods sales leaders can use when managing all this.

The Eisenhower Matrix is one of the best methods out there, if not the best. Invented by President Eisenhower, this method divides tasks and responsibilities into four categories (Victorino, 2020):

- Important and urgent: tasks that need to be done immediately
- Important but not urgent: tasks that need to be scheduled
- Urgent but not important: tasks that can be delegated
- Not urgent and not important: tasks that can be removed from the to-do list entirely

The method is simple. You list everything you must do at the start of the day. Then, you go over them and divide them into these categories. Once you know where each task squarely falls, you take action. You tend to your to-dos ASAP while scheduling specific tasks and delegating others to the most appropriate people in your team. The remainder you delete from your list because, if they are neither important nor urgent, why would they merit your time and attention?

There is a keyword in that description that you might have zeroed in on: delegation. This is another lifesaving skill that sales leaders need to have. We all have this inclination to do everything ourselves. That is where the "If you want something done right, do it yourself" comes from, after all. The thing is, sales leaders do not have the time or energy to do everything themselves. If they try to, something will either fall through the cracks or get done haphazardly. Knowing how and when to delegate is important because it frees up sales leaders' time, preventing burnout. It allows them to focus on what is important and achieve what they want. It allows them to always do their best, rather than rushing through things.

It is easy to figure out what you can delegate using the Eisenhower Matrix. It might be harder to figure out who to delegate tasks to, but there is a trick for this as well: Ask yourself who among your team has the skillset necessary to complete this task in the best possible way. Assuming this person is not overburdened with tasks, in which case you may have to reconfigure their responsibilities a bit, assigning them the work in question is the right way to go. It will not only free up your time and help you focus on your priorities, but it will also ensure that the important responsibility you are delegating gets done in a timely fashion and in the best way possible.

Sales planning is another important skill because it enables sales leaders to develop sound sales strategies. It helps them identify the target markets they want to go after and set realistic sales targets for everyone while ensuring that all these elements align with the company's larger objectives and vision. This is as much an art form as a skill, of course. Given that, it is a skill that we will be learning more about in the coming chapters, specifically.

Then there is active listening. Active listening is a listening technique where you are fully present in a conversation and hear what is being said to you. You are not thinking of something else when someone is speaking to you, even if that something else is what you are going to respond with. You are not daydreaming or planning your reaction. You are simply present and paying attention, something that's harder to do than many people realize (Cuncic, 2024). The good news is that sales leaders can take several steps to improve active listening. They can consciously pay attention to their conversation partner's nonverbal cues, the most obvious examples of which are their body language and facial expressions. They can maintain eye contact throughout the conversation, too. It is not for nothing that there is an old saying that goes, "The eyes are the windows to the soul," after all. They can ask open-ended questions throughout the conversation, refrain from interrupting the speaker, and mirror them by asking questions like "Do I understand it correctly that...?"

Techniques like these can quickly sharpen a person's active listening skills, a core asset for any sales leader. When practiced consistently, active listening sends a powerful message to both your team and your customers: *you are heard, understood, and valued.* It builds trust, strengthens relationships, and opens the door to honest, two-way communication. For customers, it often uncovers hidden needs, objections, or opportunities, critical insights that can be the deciding factor in turning a prospect into a loyal buyer. However, its value does not stop at sales. In the workplace, active listening is a proactive problem-solving tool. It helps leaders identify and address issues before they spiral into distractions, conflicts, or morale killers. The result? A team that stays motivated, energized, and laser-focused on achieving its goals.

Coaching

There is one final skill that sales leaders need to develop and sharpen, and that is their coaching skills. Coaching is a large part of any sales leader's job. To that end, they must invest in their team members' training and development. In other words, they must pursue continuous learning within the workplace. As you will recall, this is also a significant part of establishing a positive work environment.

There are several reasons why sales leaders need to invest in employee training and development. To begin with, investing in this area is a powerful way to attract top talent to the sales team. It signals that the company values growth and offers clear opportunities for self-improvement, something every ambitious professional seeks. Beyond that, it fosters job satisfaction and motivation, which naturally lead to higher employee retention, a strong indicator of a healthy, positive work environment. More importantly, though, this kind of investment allows sales leaders to identify future leaders early on and nurture them. Thus, it works for the betterment and advancement of the business that they are a part of. As if all that were not enough, it keeps sales team members more engaged and interested in their work, thereby improving productivity levels for everyone.

With all this in mind, the question is about how a sales leader can improve their coaching skills and invest in their team members in this way. For this, sales leaders need to adopt a variety of training methods. The first and likely most obvious of these methods is to give team members the right incentives. No matter how much a sales team member likes their job, they do it for one key reason: to make a living. They do their work well, and they get paid adequate compensation for it. At least, they should be adequately compensated for their efforts, because that will incentivize them to keep doing their best. Providing them with bonuses, salary increases, where appropriate, promotions, and other opportunities for advancement is also important. "You motivate team members by giving them the right incentives. You give them the recognition they deserve for their work, encouraging them to keep going. Essentially, you use a reward system that benefits everyone in the long run.

Another obvious training method is holding one-on-one meetings with sales representatives and role-playing different sales situations to help them hone their skills. This method can be beneficial to those representatives who are new to their jobs or those seeking to improve their skills in one way or another. Giving them attention like this makes it possible for them to improve themselves and motivates them further. After all, they will see that you are trying to help them improve instead of criticizing them and walking away. Appreciate the time and effort you put into this; they will likely return it.

One less obvious training method might be to integrate the sales team with other departments periodically. That way, team members can learn about how their respective business units operate and receive training in other areas.

Thus, they can pick up new skills and information that can help them in their positions in unexpected ways and experience a greater sense of belonging in the business they're a part of, especially if they forge new bonds in the process.

A similar approach may involve having thought leaders and speakers come in to work and provide team members with workshops or give speeches. Designing programs like these can allow team members to strengthen their various skills, learn new ones, and grow more confident and capable at their jobs.

A final tactic to adopt may be giving constructive criticism to sales team members. Constructive criticism is not about tearing people down. It is about pointing out what needs work so they can see it and improve it. To do that, constructive criticism needs to be delivered in a precise way. For instance, using "I feel...", "I think...", "I would recommend..." and other "I" statements is a good approach because it helps avoid blame-oriented language (Indeed Editorial Team, 2023g). Thus, it does not put the person you are talking to on the defensive. It makes them more open to hearing what you have to say and then acting on your advice.

This strategy works best when focusing on a person's behavior or actions. Focusing on specific actions would be best. That way, you can give the person you are talking to a definite idea of what they can and should improve. You will not leave any room for confusion or doubt, making things easier for all involved.

Lastly, you should always pair "negative" feedback with "positive" feedback. This way, you deliver more balanced feedback, take additional measures to prevent the person you are talking to from becoming combative, and make them more open to working on whatever they need.

CHAPTER 3
SALES STRATEGY AND PLANNING

Opportunities are usually disguised as hard work, so most people don't recognize them.

−Ann Landers

As you know, one of the core skills every great sales leader must master is sales planning. It works hand-in-hand with sales strategy, a term we have referenced several times already. However, what do these terms mean? How does a sales leader effectively plan sales? Moreover, how can they build a strong, results-driven sales strategy?

To answer the first question, a sales strategy is a detailed blueprint that outlines your sales team's structure and responsibilities, your organizational goals, the market data you have gathered, your customer personas, and other critical information that guides your approach. Your sales strategy is the overarching approach you will use to achieve your long-term sales goals and overall objectives. Your sales plan is the flexible, action-oriented plan you devise to achieve that long-term objective, as well as your various long and short-term sales goals, which, ideally, should build up and lead you to the overall aim.

If you think that sounds rather complicated, you are correct. Luckily, we can make creating a sales plan and strategy significantly less complicated by breaking it down into a series of steps, starting with sales planning. Before we do that, though, let us first understand why sales leaders need sales strategies. Wouldn't it be faster and easier to go to a prospective customer and pitch them your product? You'd think so, but this will backfire on you often. Sure, you might talk to more people each day if you decide not to set aside time for strategizing, but you will not be able to make personalized pitches to those you talk to. You will not understand their needs, so you will not be able to show them that the product you are selling meets those needs.

This is one reason why sales leaders must choose a sales strategy and develop a sales plan that aligns with it. Some plans and strategies, such as sales plans, allow sales leaders to plan, anticipate potential problems, and devise solutions in advance. Sales strategies and planning also help sales leaders identify and speak to their target customers directly. This understandably results in more sales. Add to that the fact that sales strategies help sales leaders position their business or brand in the existing market in a way that can capitalize on the current and emerging trends.

Sales Planning

All that is good, but how can sales leaders create effective plans? This process starts with deciding on the kind of sales strategy they want to adopt. Overall, there are five types of sales strategies that sales leaders might adopt. These are:

- value-based selling
- consultative selling
- solution selling
- challenger selling
- Situation, problem, implication, need (SPIN) selling

Most sales leaders consider **value-based selling** to be the most effective strategy among these. So, let us start by focusing on that. Sales leaders tend to favor value-based selling because value-based selling is incredibly effective. It appears directly to the customer, that is, the individual, and therefore often results in more sales. Hence, the strategy is customer-focused. It puts their needs and wants at the forefront. This makes it easy for sales teams to appeal to those needs and wants, translating to more sales.

Just because value-based selling is highly effective, though, does not mean it is the best strategy out of all that's available to sales leaders. There is not a "best" strategy, at least not generally speaking. What works well for one business, brand, or company may not apply to another, meaning the term "best" is highly subjective. Value-based selling may be the most fitting for one specific brand, but it might be different for another. Luckily, a sales leader who feels value-based selling is not the ideal route can opt for a different sales strategy, like consultative selling.

Consultative selling is a strategy where sales representatives act as advisors to customers. To that end, they present various solutions to their customers or focus on educating them on why their product is right for them. In this role, salespersons become experts in their industries and adopt this role wholeheartedly.

Consultative selling is quite different from solution selling.

Solution selling is a strategy that has salespeople perform deep dives into their prospective customers' pain points and values. Salespeople provide their customers with solutions to those unique pain points and problems through the product or service they are selling. Thus, they make value-based propositions to their customers. In this regard, solution selling is like value-based selling. The key difference between the two methodologies is that solution selling is a highly data-driven approach focusing on specific, concrete issues. On the other hand, value-based selling is more general and more about understanding the customer base rather than their pain points exclusively.

Challenger selling is a sales strategy that involves identifying and analyzing the behaviors, tactics, and closing techniques of top-performing sales representatives. Sales leaders then train the rest of their team to adopt these proven methods. The goal is to equip all sales representatives with the same effective strategies, ensuring consistency and improved performance across the board. While the strategy can be very effective, it can also be inflexible. Market trends and needs may change after all, rendering the sales techniques that are being taught to entire sales teams ineffective. If this is not recognized on time, the situation can affect the entire sales team. However, if identified on time, sales leaders can go back to observing their representatives for a while until they discover what other methods and techniques work among their customer base. They can then focus on teaching those methods to their sales teams, ensuring the sales department's continued success in the long term.

Finally, there is **SPIN selling**. SPIN selling stands for

- situation
- problem
- implication
- need-payoff

The SPIN selling strategy begins with a sales leader defining the situation and problem that customers or potential customers are having. They then explain what this situation and these problems imply for the customer. Having obtained a thorough understanding of matters in this way, they finally list all the needed payoffs that they, meaning the sales leader, the brand, and the customer, would get by meeting the customers' needs and solving their problems. To do this, sales leaders need to ask the right questions. Otherwise, they will need help to determine customers' problems and situational needs accurately. As a result, they will not be able to solve problems on their own or meet their needs. Of course, this strategy also necessitates sales leaders asking their questions at the right time when they are talking to customers and building a relationship with them. Otherwise, they will not be able to get the answers they need, at least not enough to devise a sufficient plan of action.

You may have noticed that all these strategies prioritize one thing, first and foremost: understanding customer needs, problems, and pain points. This is because whether a sale happens ultimately depends on the customer. Your ability to convince them that they need or want a product is crucial. When selling a product, you want to convince them that they "need" it. This is because people's needs are things they are willing to spend their hard-earned money on. Their wants, however, are things they can skip. The best way to convince someone they need a product is to make sure it solves a pain point in their lives. That lies at the heart of the strategies we have covered so far.

While the five sales strategies available to sales leaders may share similar goals, each takes a distinct approach to the sales process and defines different relationship dynamics between the sales representative and the customer. For instance, **consultative selling** positions the salesperson as an expert or advisor, aiming to educate the customer. This creates a dynamic like that of a teacher and student, with the salesperson guiding the conversation. In contrast, **value-**

based selling fosters a more balanced relationship, placing the salesperson and customer on equal footing, with an emphasis on collaboration and mutual respect.

To choose or set a sales strategy, sales leaders need to decide what methodology and dynamic would work best for their sales teams. To determine this, they will need to form a thorough understanding of both the brand they represent and the customers they are dealing with. Hence, setting a sales strategy follows some specific steps:

1. Taking stock of your resources

2. Establishing a value proposition

3. Creating a customer persona

4. Structuring your strategic plan

A sales leader's first step when putting together a sales strategy is to take stock of the available resources. This is a logical first step because it prevents sales leaders from developing strategies that will deplete their resources over time and ultimately prove unsustainable for them. To be clear, "resources" does not just refer to the budget available to sales teams. It also refers to the salespeople, who constitute the department's human capital. In addition to that, it includes the tools that sales teams have at their disposal, the processes they use, and the incentives that support them. These are all resources sales leaders need to evaluate before setting a sales strategy for their teams (*How Do You Plan and Manage Sales Resources?* LinkedIn 2023).

To that end, sales leaders need to ask themselves specific questions, like

- What resources do my sales teams have access to?
- How can I help my sales teams achieve their sales

goals?
- What obstacles might my sales teams face, and how can I help solve them?
- Do I have enough salespeople in my teams, and do they have enough of the right tools to execute the strategy I'm developing?

As sales leaders ask such questions, they must consider various factors, like their sales teams' size, how they're structured, what territories they operate in, and sales representatives' skills and respective roles. These factors will play a part in how their questions are answered.

Once a sales leader has the complete picture of the available resources, they can move on to the next step, establishing a value proposition. Simply put, a value proposition is the unique selling point of a product or service. It's what sales leaders try to communicate to customers and prospective customers. Writing a good value proposition starts with identifying the main problem that a customer is having. This will require doing some research. At this stage, sales leaders must speak to customer service representatives, sales team members, and marketing specialists to gather as much information as possible. By doing so, they will be able to understand customer problems in-depth and from various angles (Coleman, 2023).

Next, sales leaders must identify and describe the main benefits of their products or services. They should strive to describe what makes those benefits valuable to the customer. More importantly, they should endeavor to connect the benefits they have identified to the problems the customer is having. In other words, they should articulate how their product or service will solve customers' problems or meet their needs.

All this might sound like a big task, but sales leaders have specific tools to make these processes much easier. One of these tools is called SWOT Analysis, which is an acronym that stands for

- strengths
- weaknesses
- opportunities
- threats (Kenton, 2023)

The "strengths" in this analysis refer to the benefits of the product or service a sales leader is trying to sell to customers. Meanwhile, weaknesses refer to areas of improvement that prevent sales teams from selling a service or product at the optimum level. Opportunities stand for favorable outside conditions, like market trends, that can be taken advantage of to help sales teams sell their service or product. Finally, threats refer to the various factors that can hinder sales processes. As an example of what threats may look like, say that you are the sales leader of a cosmetic company. Many of your products are made with special ingredients only found in a specific region of the Amazon Rainforest. If forest fires suddenly broke out in that region, this would put a key ingredient at stake for you. It would, therefore, put your products at risk, too.

This is a rather extreme example, but concrete enough to get the idea across. In any case, the SWOT analysis usually unfolds in five steps. The first is to determine your objective. For a sales leader, that may be selling a new product developed by their company. The second step is to gather all the data you can, focus specifically on the four factors: strengths, weaknesses, opportunities, and threats, that go into the SWOT analysis. The best strategy to adopt in this information-gathering phase is to talk to as many people as possible. That way, you can see these four factors from as varied perspectives as humanly possible. This is essential because having more varied perspectives means obtaining more diverse, value-adding contributions.

The next step of the SWOT analysis is to start generating ideas. These ideas should use the strengths and opportunities identified while accounting for the weaknesses and threats that've been spotted. A brainstorming session can be fantastic for this. Once you have come up with a whole stock of ideas, you can refine your findings by weighing them against one another and narrowing things down until you have the perfect value propositions. Some examples of significant value propositions to make note of might be (Shewan, 2023):

- Uber: The most innovative way to get around.
- Slack: Be more productive at work with less effort.
- LessAccounting: Bookkeeping without the hassle.
- CrazyEgg: Website behavior tracking at an unbeatable price.

After identifying their unique value proposition, a sales leader can move on to creating a customer persona. A customer persona is a profile of the ideal customer who buys the product or service you are selling. The more you understand this customer, the more you will be able to cater to their needs and solve their problems. Thus, the more you can sell (Needle, 2023), the more data you will gather on your customers. Customer personas, then, make it easier for you to generate "leads". It also helps you optimize demand and nurture the "leads" you get. At the same time, it allows you to customize your marketing campaigns according to your ideal customers and tailor messaging for them.

Naturally, this is all contingent on your ability to create an accurate customer persona. The first thing you need to do with this is to fill out your ideal customer's basic demographic information. This means knowing the answer to questions like

- How old is my customer?
- What is their gender?
- Where are they based?
- What is their income level?
- How do they prefer communicating with others (e.g., phone calls, emails, social media, etc.)?
- What industries are they in?
- What is their family situation like?
- What kind of lifestyle are they leading?

When you finish your customer's basic demographic information, you can move on to their motivations. In other words, you can focus on their professional or personal goals. What motivates these customers? What unique problems are they experiencing? What needs do they have, and which ones are not met? What stands in the way of their ability to meet their goals? What is their personality like?

Determining the answer to such questions is important for two reasons. First, they allow you to tailor your value propositions for those customers specifically. Second, they prepare you for the sales conversations with these customers. They help you anticipate objections that customers may make to buying what you are selling and develop compelling counterarguments in advance, for example. They help you find the proper evidence to present in your talks. For example, someone who is very scientifically minded will not be persuaded to buy something because you have told them a touching story about it. Come at them with scientific evidence as to why they need the product you are selling, and their response will likely be very different.

Having done all this, you can turn to the last step of the process: crafting the right messaging for your target customer. That done, you can, at last, start structuring your strategic plan. Your data lets you decide which strategy would work best for you. You can then begin assembling your plan, which will entail creating an outline of actionable tasks specific to your sales team. There is one last factor you will need to consider before crafting your outline, though, and that is the market you are operating in. Markets are volatile and ever-changing entities. They are often subject to different trends and are impacted by the economy. Knowing the current state of the market can allow you to take advantage of ongoing and emerging trends, identify niches you can exploit, and take protective measures in times of hardship. However, being able to do all this requires knowing how to use yet another tool: a target market analysis.

Target Market Analysis

A target market analysis tool can help you formulate solid, effective strategic sales plans. Such an analysis can be defined as a thorough evaluation of the market in which your product or services will exist. Performing a target market analysis requires identifying your target audience. Luckily, you will already have figured this out by creating a customer persona. Based on that, you can write a concrete description of your business in the industry. You will then be able to evaluate the target market itself, which will entail testing market results, investigating your lead time, and performing a good competitive analysis.

So, you have created a customer persona and know precisely who you will be targeting. That means you have a fair bit of data on hand. You can use this data to describe your industry, which serves as your starting point. Your description should include the market's size, growth potential, and outlook. As you may have noticed, this information may not necessarily have been obtained while creating your customer persona. If so, then you may have to conduct further research.

The additional research you do when working on your target market analysis will give you a complete picture of your market. This picture should include:

- your target market's age
- their gender
- income level
- geographic location
- lifestyle
- needs, wants, and preferences
- the market size
- the market's purchasing potential
- your customers' motivations
- your marketing ideas (Indeed Editorial Team, 2023c)

If you have all this data, you can focus on product testing. For example, you can do beta tests among a select group of customers and hold surveys to see how your target market responds to your product or service. Once those tests and surveys are completed, you can compile their results into a concise report. You can also investigate your business's lead time as you do this. Your lead time is the duration it takes for your brand to process and ship a product, and the time it takes for the customer to get hold of it. As a rule, you want to keep the lead time as short as possible without compromising the quality of the product, of course. However, please note that the lead time for bulk orders may vary from that of individual orders.

The final part of a target market analysis is the competitive analysis. Doing a competitive analysis requires identifying your competitors in the market. What products and services are they offering? What are you offering that they do not? What do you do better than they do or offer that they do not? What do they seem to do better than you? What are their customers praising and criticizing them for? Identifying these things can help you determine ways to outperform and outshine your competitors. You can then focus your strategic plans on these avenues. Furthermore, you can anticipate future challenges and devise innovative ways to overcome them quickly.

Goal Setting

Doing a target market analysis helps you with something pretty essential: setting the right goals for the strategic plan you are devising by taking all the necessary and accurate information into account. Goal setting is a massive part of any sound strategic plan. As you devise a plan, you want to set the right long- and short-term goals. This will ensure that the plan you put in place is ultimately doable.

While goal setting may seem easy at first, it can quickly become very complicated. You see, many people tend to overestimate things like their work speed. So they end up setting unrealistic goals, thinking they will be able to accomplish them. Soon enough, they find out that they were mistaken. While such a tendency toward overestimation might not lead to drastic consequences concerning personal goals, it can lead to dire ones in the sales world. Setting unrealistic and, therefore, unachievable goals for sales teams as part of sales strategies and plans can be disastrous for all involved. Knowing how to set the right goals correctly is essential for sales leaders. The question is how.

The answer to that question is pretty simple: by setting SMART goals. SMART goals are another acronym that stands for (Leonard & Watts, 2022)

- specific
- measurable
- achievable
- relevant
- time-bound

Your goals need to be specific because specific goals give your sales team members explicit direction on what to do and how to do it. It leaves no room for confusion, boosting everyone's ability to get things done. Goals likewise must be measurable. That means they must be quantifiable so that you know exactly when you've achieved them and can move on to the next one. "Be successful," for instance, isn't a measurable goal because success is a subjective term that hasn't been defined in this sentence. "Sell ten new subscriptions in three days," on the other hand, is a very measurable goal, as it comes with both solid instructions and firm benchmarks.

Goals must, additionally, be achievable. Say that you have set a sales quota as a goal. If your sales team lacks the necessary resources to meet a quota, that goal will not be achieved. However, it might be a good goal for later, when you have the necessary resources.

What about relevance? A relevant goal aligns with your ultimate objective. Along the way, you will set many short-term goals, but each one must directly support and move you closer to your long-term goal. Achieving them should take you to your overall aim, step by step. Every goal in your strategic plan should be worth the fight and achievable. If it cannot be achieved, drop it. Focus your energy on the goals that matter, the ones that will move the needle and take you where you want to go.

Finally, goals must be time-bound, meaning they must come with deadlines. This is vital for productivity's sake. It is the only way to ensure the tasks that need to be completed are finished on time, without delays, procrastination, and stress.

Always setting SMART goals for the sales team is good business practice for sales leaders. It is not the only one. Sales leaders can adopt other business practices to heighten team members' ability to meet their goals. One such practice is to write determined SMART goals, especially team goals, in a visible location that can be seen daily by all. For instance, a whiteboard in the office would be great for this. Writing down goals like this makes them feel more real to everyone. It is something that reminds everyone of their aims and, therefore, proves motivating. It ensures nothing is forgotten or done halfway, to boot.

Another business practice for sales leaders to consider is sharing their SMART goals with all relevant individuals. This includes the members of their sales team, department heads who need to be made aware of them—like the head of marketing, for instance, and other stakeholders. This fosters an understanding that everyone shares these goals, creating a sense of unity and belonging across departments. Thus, it increases everyone's motivation and commitment to work harder. It also makes it easier for team members to support one another in the long and short term.

Sales leaders also must evaluate their teams' progress regularly. Sometimes, despite our best efforts, we set goals that prove hard to meet. There can be any number of reasons for this. Sudden changes in the market or new market trends might be another. Another might be structural changes to the company you are a part of, which would disrupt anyone's focus and motivation for a time. Whatever the case, evaluating goals regularly is a good idea because it allows sales leaders to identify potential problems quickly and adjust their goals. This is an excellent way of ensuring that chosen goals are flexible, realistic, and achievable, especially within the timeframes allotted to them.

One last thing sales leaders can do regarding SMART goals is to celebrate the milestones that their sales teams and representatives achieve. Celebrating milestones is important because it allows you to keep track of the progress that has been made. It motivates everyone and helps them do their best. It keeps people from feeling stuck in place, which can easily happen when you do not celebrate milestones because progress is not always easy to see for all. All in all, celebrating milestones, no matter how small, is an encouraging act for all, with the added benefit of contributing to the positive work environment you have created for your sales team.

Territory Management

The final step in sales planning and strategy is territory management. Territory management refers to how you plan and execute the sales strategies you have decided on in different territories. It is important because different territories have different landscapes and needs. These needs and the unique characteristics of those landscapes inevitably change your approach to the market you are dealing with and how the customers in those territories view and respond to the product or service you are offering them (Coleman, 2023).

Your first order of business regarding territory management is to define the markets you are dealing with. This will ultimately allow you to determine and set up new territories and assign various sales leaders to them. Your next step is to evaluate the different accounts that sales teams will be handling in those territories and markets. This evaluation can be either qualitative or quantitative, depending on the product or service. The idea is to determine the value of each account so that they can determine which ones and in which territories are most important and, therefore, should be prioritized.

This will make the next step, territory assessment, much easier. Territory assessment means determining the value and potential of a specific territory. Sales leaders should approach this step with their sales managers and teams, who know these territories best from firsthand experience. They understand not only the key players but also the ongoing and emerging trends. Their insights can be invaluable in guiding practical territory assessment and management. The next and most important step in territory management is to determine the strengths and weaknesses of the sales representatives operating in the various territories you serve. A SWOT analysis can come in very handy at this stage. By conducting such an assessment, sales leaders can identify the "ideal" sales representatives and teams for different territories. They can assign territories to the salespeople and teams whose strengths are best suited for them. Thus, they will be able to empower the representatives and teams in question, increasing both their motivation and productivity levels.

Sales leaders should make it a habit to review their goals periodically and adjust them as circumstances evolve, flexibility is key to staying effective. The same principle applies to territory plans. These plans should be revisited regularly and refined as needed. This involves analyzing sales performance across regions and monitoring key metrics. Taking a proactive approach helps identify inefficiencies early on, allowing leaders to address potential issues before they escalate. It will help them identify opportunities they have yet to explore.

CHAPTER 4
SALES PERFORMANCE MANAGEMENT

———◆———

Don't watch the clock; do what it does. Keep going.

–Sam Levenson

A sales leader's job is multifaceted. One facet is recruiting talent and putting together the best sales teams. Another is managing those teams' performance. It ensures everyone performs at optimal levels at all times. It is using the right incentives to motivate and encourage team members.

Similarly, it is identifying instances of underperformance, getting to the root of them quickly, and addressing them post-haste. As you can gather from all that, managing sales teams' performance is a nuanced task. For one, it requires accurately evaluating teams' and people's performance. For another, it requires understanding psychology to a degree so that you can motivate people effectively and fix instances of underperformance permanently. A sales leader who wants to do a good job managing sales performance must master both of these arts, starting with the first.

Key Performance Indicators (Kpis)

Evaluating a sales team's performance is not always easy, especially without the right tools. In sales, it is essential to have clear, effective benchmarks to track progress and determine if goals are being met. One of the most important tools sales leaders rely on for this is the use of key performance indicators, or KPIs. KPIs are essentially quantifiable measurements that sales leaders use to evaluate sales teams' and team members' performance in the long term. They constitute a vital tool for refining the strategies developed for sales teams, ensuring that all financial and operational goals are met, and that all team members perform at the maximum level.

KPIs are essential tools for sales teams, enabling four key functions: collecting, storing, cleaning, and synthesizing data. In simple terms, KPIs gather information, extract key insights, draw accurate conclusions, and deliver these findings to sales leaders, equipping them with the data they need to make informed decisions. KPIs' goal is to communicate their conclusions to sales leaders succinctly, as those conclusions will allow said leaders to make informed strategic decisions for their teams and the future of their companies (Twin, 2024).

As it happens, there are four different kinds of KPIs. They are:

- strategic
- operational
- functional
- leading/lagging

Strategic KPIs provide a high-level overview of how the company is performing overall, offering a snapshot of its broader progress. In contrast, operational KPIs track performance on a more regular basis, such as monthly progress toward specific objectives. Functional KPIs focus on individual departments, for example, monitoring the performance of the sales team. Then there are leading and lagging KPIs: leading indicators look ahead, measuring activities that can influence future outcomes, while lagging indicators reflect results from past events.

Just as there are different kinds of KPIs, there are also different types. These types differ from one another based on their focus. Financial KPIs, for example, focus on profit margins and revenue. Customer experience KPIs are related to customer satisfaction and retention. Marketing KPIs are all about making marketing campaigns as effective as possible.

Out of all these different KPI types, however, the one that sales leaders are primarily concerned with is sales KPIs. Sales KPIs often incorporate financial metrics to provide deeper insight into the effectiveness of the sales process. A key financial KPI commonly used by sales leaders is Customer Acquisition Cost (CAC), which represents the total marketing and sales expense required to acquire a new customer. CAC is typically evaluated alongside another important metric, Customer Lifetime Value (CLV), which estimates the total revenue a customer is expected to generate over the course of their relationship with the brand (Twin, 2024). CAC is measured against CLV because it shows sales leaders the effectiveness of their customer acquisition efforts.

There are many other sales KPIs besides these two. One is the average dollar value for new contracts. As you might have guessed from the name, this equals the average size of a new agreement. Often, sales departments have a desired threshold for this. So, sales leaders try to meet that threshold, which changes depending on the size of a customer. There is a difference between one company being a customer of another and a middle-income person being the customer.

Then there is the number of "leads" engaged. This KPI

tracks the number of potential contractors contacted. Sales leaders can divide this KPI into narrower segments, like in-person visits, phone calls, emails, or other contact methods. Finally, there is the average conversion time, which is the duration it takes to turn a prospective customer into an actual one.

All these KPIs yield invaluable data for sales leaders to use. They typically use them to craft KPI reports. To craft an effective KPI report, a sales leader must first determine their overall goal. When that is done, they must list their SMART goals and tie them together with their KPIs (Indeed Editorial Team, 2023a). This way, they can ensure their KPIs are as concrete, easy to follow, execute, and realistic as possible. KPIs that do not fit this definition will not be useful to sales leaders or teams.

When you have married all your goals to your KPIs, you can draft an outline showing what your KPI report will look like. Your outline should start with a brief introduction, stating the report's goal. A description of the KPIs collected should follow this, the data they have yielded, and any charts that may illustrate the information they present. As you draft your outline, you should consider the order in which you want to present the collected information. That way, you can perfect your report's narrative before you write it.

Your outline must include concrete definitions of your KPIs. These definitions must include your reasoning as to why you chose those specific KPIs, how you tracked the information in question, and what relevant terms, like lead time, for example, mean. The KPIs themselves must then follow these definitions. Once you have added all the data in, your report will officially be complete, though you can proofread it a few times and review the information you have presented. You can then use this report to do any number of things, like

- inform your department about specific problems you have identified and that need to be fixed.
- refine your sales strategy based on the new data and insights you have obtained.
- hold employees and peers accountable for their actions.
- ensure goals are being met effectively and figure out how they can be met if this is not the case.
- set achievable objectives for your sales team and monitor the progress that's being made (Twin, 2024).

Performance Reviews

Another highly effective tool you can use to monitor and manage sales teams' performance is to conduct performance reviews. Sales leaders must conduct performance reviews regularly to understand how their sales teams meet expectations and achieve goals. A sales performance review is an annual evaluation where sales leaders can discuss team members' performance, productivity, goals, and overall career development. They are great for discussing how someone's performance can be improved, possible promotions, pay raises, and other advancement opportunities (Indeed Editorial Team, 2022).

A good sales leader must create an outline before starting a performance review. Think of it like this: If you were going to give an important speech onstage, you would not just head to the podium and wing it. You should prepare talking points instead. Preparing such talking points before performance reviews is a good idea, as it clarifies exactly what you want to accomplish in each review. It helps you focus on the key points you want to discuss, quantify your objectives, and establishes how someone's performance and quality of work can be improved. It also makes it easier to stay on topic during reviews.

Before you start a performance review, you must ensure you have the right data. This can mean anything, from sales figures to customer reviews. Out of all this data, you will want to focus on key sales performance metrics, such as total sales figures and revenue. These constitute concrete metrics that you can use to evaluate team members' performance and pinpoint areas for improvement quickly and accurately. They have the added benefit of making it easier for you to discuss sales results, focusing on individual sales members' contributions.

Addressing areas for improvement is a vital part of performance reviews. It is also a delicate matter; you cannot simply point out what is not working and leave it at that. Instead, you must provide team members with opportunities for improvement. You must address areas of concern in a compassionate and understanding way, too. There can be a myriad of reasons why someone's sales performance is down, after all. For instance, if a team member has recently lost a family member, the loss will impact them psychologically. It will, therefore, also impact their performance, at least for a time. A good sales leader knows how to be understanding during this period of grief. Therefore, they can bring the matter to the team members' attention without judgment or condemnation. At the same time, they can provide them with solutions to help them improve. Giving them a short while to get back on their feet, for example, and helping them manage their workload for that period could be one option to pursue.

Sales leaders should not just address areas for improvement in their reviews. They should talk about what team members are doing right, too. Studies show that employees who only receive negative feedback are 63% more likely to leave their companies (McGlauflin & Abrams, 2023). Seventeen percent of the employees who ultimately leave their place of employment cite their performance reviews and the overwhelmingly negative feedback as their primary reason for leaving. Providing positive feedback while addressing areas for improvement can prevent this in your sales teams. As a result, it can boost both employee satisfaction and retention at the same time.

Performance reviews work best when sales leaders set individual and group goals for their sales team members in the reviews themselves (Indeed Editorial Team, 2022). This is contingent on those goals being realistic and achievable, of course. Once more, SMART goals are the way to go with this. Providing team members with opportunities for self-assessment is also a great way to improve the effectiveness of reviews. This allows team members to share their input, their feelings about their work, and their contributions. This gets everyone to reflect on their experiences as part of the sales team, enhancing their sense of belonging. It enables them to identify ways they can improve themselves and increase their motivation, productivity, and engagement levels at work, too.

Finally, sales leaders should offer guidance to team members and ask for their feedback. Offering guidance to team members who need it helps them improve themselves more quickly. It also feeds into the positive relationship you are trying to forge with team members and enhances your vital communication skills, as you have seen. Offering guidance puts sales leaders in mentorship positions where they can motivate team members to perform at their best and achieve success. Asking for feedback further improves sales leader-team member relationships by encouraging openness and honesty and building rapport. It makes team members feel that their opinions matter. Consequently, this sense of value and validation creates a more positive work environment for all.

Contrary to what you might think, a performance review does not end when the meeting ends. This is because sales leaders have to check in on individual team members after their performance reviews, particularly if they are struggling and need to improve in specific areas. Say that you met with a team member and devised a game plan for them to improve their sales figures. As part of the plan, you set specific goals for the salesperson. After your initial meeting, it is important to follow up regularly to assess whether the plan is on track and the goals are being met. If everything is progressing well, you can step back and allow the team members to continue confidently. However, if the targets are not being met, it may be necessary to have a follow-up conversation to address the underperformance and take appropriate action.

Managing Underperformance

Sales leaders will undoubtedly have to deal with instances of underperformance occasionally. Some people would be inclined to let underperforming salespeople go immediately. However, that is not a good idea, as there may be many reasons someone is underperforming. If you find out the root cause of someone's underperformance, you will be able to solve it. Thus, you will be able to help that team member become as productive as they used to be, if not more, in no time. This will often be far easier than letting team members go and trying to find suitable replacements. Additionally, letting salespeople go at the first sign of underperformance sets a bad precedent for other team members. It gives them the message that they will be let go of the moment they stumble and fall. This lowers their satisfaction levels with their jobs while increasing the stress and anxiety they experience at work. That, in turn, makes them more inclined to look for other jobs, ones where they will be treated with greater understanding. Such a policy would be detrimental to employee retention, which is why sales leaders should avoid it.

The main thing sales leaders need to remember is that everyone hits hurdles sometimes. This includes salespeople. Chastising salespeople when their performance levels suffer because they have come across an obstacle will not help them improve. Likewise, letting salespeople go at the first sign of underperformance will not help the sales team. It will not motivate other team members to keep working hard, either. However, taking measures to help the underperforming team members will significantly help them and the team.

There are a variety of measures sales leaders can and should take to manage underperformance. The first step is to schedule a meeting with the underperforming individual to address the situation at hand (Gallo, 2014). When setting up a meeting, a team member or a sales leader must start by informing them of the purpose of the meeting. That way, the team member in question can prepare for the meeting and not feel ambushed when sitting down to talk. As meetings addressing underperformance can be delicate, sales leaders must choose a private environment to hold them, like their personal office space. Ideally, this space should be free from prying eyes, and somewhere, they will not be overheard. That way, discussing the issue and its underlying causes will be easier for the team members. In a private setting, a sales leader can invite the team members they are talking to, encouraging them to share their thoughts and feelings honestly while offering them support throughout the conversation.

This is all a prelude to the meeting, of course. The actual meeting is another matter. When a sales leader enters a meeting to address someone's underperformance, they must avoid playing the blame game. That can be not easy to do, but it is essential. Assigning blame in underperformance meetings is a sure way to put the team member on the defensive. It is a move that makes them less likely to take responsibility for their actions or inaction. It is something that can drive them to come up with excuses. When you assign blame, you essentially guarantee that the things you say will not be heard or taken to heart. So, the meeting proves pointless, and nothing changes at all.

Sales leaders need to opt for another route if they want to manage underperformance successfully. They want to clearly state what they have observed and explain why it's an issue. They want to relay their concerns and invite the individual to share their thoughts on the matter to help them understand why this problem has arisen. Unearthing the problem behind a team member's underperformance will enable you to fix it. Fix the problem, and that team member's underperformance will solve itself, and things will return to how they used to be.

There can be many reasons someone is suddenly underperforming, as said before. It might be that a team member is overworked and has too many tasks to focus on; for example, the issue should go away once their workload has been revised. They might be dealing with a family matter that is proving to be distracting for them, so providing them with some additional support may be helpful. There might, alternatively, be a wholly different reason behind the problem at hand. Whatever the issue is, the sales leader's primary focus in these meetings has to be on solving it. So, how does one discover the root cause of underperformance?

A sales leader can only determine the root cause of such issues if they work with the underperforming team members. That is why they have these underperformance meetings in the first place. These meetings are venues where they can explore various ideas, ask team members' opinions, and be prepared to redefine responsibilities, workloads, work arrangements, training, and more. They are the places where they can ask team members to come up with helpful ideas of their own, make helpful suggestions, and share their concerns with them so that those can be addressed.

Once sales leaders and team members have identified possible solutions, they can create realistic action plans. These action plans must clarify the team members' new or amended responsibilities, what is expected of them moving forward, and the strategy that has been jointly decided on. It must also include a follow-up meeting date between the sales leader and the team member. The aim of this follow-up meeting must be to assess progress. Sales leaders should monitor the performance of the team members in question periodically, leading to the official follow-up meeting. They should make a point to provide them with constructive feedback and positive reinforcement to maintain their motivation and determination and help them as they work to improve their performance.

Sales leaders should additionally keep a thorough, written record of everything, from their observations to what was discussed and said in underperformance meetings. These records will serve as a valuable reference tool for future use. They will also be helpful if a team member's performance levels do not improve despite the changes that have been made, especially if the employee's performance declines to the point where they need to be let go.

CHAPTER 5
SALES PROCESS OPTIMIZATION

Companies should be selling ideas more than benefits. Sell Ideas. Not stuff.

–Aaron Ross

Sales leaders are not just in charge of assembling and managing impressive sales teams; they also have other responsibilities, like finding new ways to optimize their sales processes. "Optimizing sales processes" is a fancy term that means reducing costs while increasing revenue, thereby maximizing the organization's profit (Indeed Editorial Team, 2023e). Sales leaders can optimize their sales processes in several ways. Some ways, however, are more effective than others. What are the most effective optimization methods that sales leaders can use, and how can they use them?

Sales Funnel Management

The first highly effective optimization method sales leaders can use is sales funnel management. Picture a funnel in your mind. A typical funnel is wide at the top and narrow at the base. The top of this funnel represents the pool of potential customers a sales leader will target (Tyre, 2023). As potential customers move down the funnel, the structure will get narrower, which means various potential customers will drop out. Essentially, they are eliminated from the funnel based on specific requirements. The potential customers who reach the bottom of the funnel are converted into actual customers. In essence, a sales funnel is the process through which the "leads" found by the sales teams are turned into actual sales.

The sales process can typically be divided into three stages, which means that the sales funnel can be divided into three segments:

- awareness
- qualified lead
- decision-making and closing

Awareness is at the very top of your funnel. During this stage, sales teams capture potential customers' attention and draw their interest in the product or service they are trying to sell. It is when they start establishing a relationship with these prospects and use a variety of methods to do so, like

- content marketing, which is a process that entails publishing visual and written content with the intent of capturing potential customers' attention and getting them interested in the brand, creating the content (Baker, 2023).

- lead generation forms, which are web forms such as newsletters and registration forms, can capture different individuals' emails and information (Broadley, 2024).

- social media campaigns, which are promotional campaigns that are launched to target potential customers on various social media sites like Twitter, which has over 365 million users worldwide; Facebook, which has more than two billion users worldwide; and Instagram, which has around one billion users worldwide (Baker, 2021).

- sales prospecting, which is the process of identifying and then reaching out to potential customers and turning them into qualifying "leads" (Davies, 2022).

- webinars, which are online seminars and, therefore, a tool that is similar to content marketing in that they can prove to be exciting and engaging ways of hooking new potential customers and drawing their attention to a brand (Birt, 2023).

Efforts such as these move the sales process to the next stage in the funnel: the qualified lead. At this stage, sales leaders and teams provide prospective customers with more information about their brand, product, or service to help them make an informed decision. To that end, they again use a variety of tools. One of these tools is free trials, which are popular for online services and apps. Many apps like Spotify, Hulu, Amazon Prime, and Audible have free trials that last a week. The idea is to get customers to experience the glory of the app in question and, thus, get them hooked enough to be willing to pay a monthly or yearly subscription fee.

Another all-too-often-used tool is case studies and testimonials. Testimonials are essentially evidence that proves the product a salesperson is trying to sell is as good and effective as they claim. They are tools that often use the power of storytelling, which usually proves more effective in convincing people to invest in a product than facts, figures, and statistics can. Such facts and statistics can also be convenient, especially when targeting more scientifically minded customers. They can provide salespeople with undeniable evidence of their claims, appealing to prospective customers' more logical side.

Salespeople can also use price quotes and fixed prices for specific products and services. Suppliers often provide potential buyers with price quotes on the condition that they are valid only for a set window of time (Indeed Editorial Team, 2023f). Price quotes work because they make it easy for prospective buyers to compare brands offering similar products or services. Likewise, they make it possible for them to plan their budgets and make buying decisions more quickly and easily. For sales teams, quotes improve sales relations, thereby increasing the likelihood of converting a prospective customer to an actual one and building trust between them by allowing for transparency.

The final bottom segment of the funnel is the decision-making and closing stage. This is when sales leaders and teams employ their final tactics to get prospective customers to purchase the product or service they are trying to sell. The tactics that sales teams use at this stage can vary. Offering prospective customers discounts, for instance, might be one tactic. Entering contract negotiations might be another. Still, other tactics may include customer onboarding, upselling, and cross-selling.

Customer onboarding can be defined as teaching new customers why the product or service is valuable to them (Bishop, 2024). Customer onboarding can either take place when a customer first agrees to buy a product or service or when they use it for the first time and see its benefits for themselves. The idea behind onboarding is to get customers to realize the value of a product or service as early as possible, thereby converting them into lifelong followers.

As for upselling and cross-selling, the former is convincing an existing customer to pay for a more expensive version of a product or service you've sold them. Meanwhile, the latter sells a different product or service to a customer who has already bought one of your products or services. An app getting an existing customer to sign up for the premium version of their subscription is a great example of upselling. A cosmetic brand getting customers to buy their makeup, skincare, or haircare products is a good example of cross-selling.

The steps we've covered so far, awareness, qualified lead, and decision-making and closing, are simply the phases involved in the sales funnel itself. The steps that sales leaders take to manage sales funnels successfully are entirely different from these. To manage a sales funnel successfully, sales leaders must:

- capture "leads".
- qualify "leads".
- engage the qualified prospects within the funnel.
- move opportunities through the funnel.
- re-engage lost "leads".
- keep evaluating the funnel and its performance (DealHub Experts, 2024).

The first thing a sales leader must do to manage their sales funnel is to focus on capturing "leads". This means focusing on capturing the attention of their ideal customers, whom they should have identified by building customer personas and doing target market research. Now that they know who to target, sales leaders can contact them through several means. They can cold-call and email "leads", turn to content marketing to bring "leads", pay for traditional ads, or use referrals. to name a few options.

Once sales leaders have gathered a pool of prospects through such methods, they will have to qualify their "leads". That means identifying the prospects in the ideal position to buy the product or service. For example, several of the "leads" may not be ready to make a purchase. Some of them will not be able to buy because of economic constraints. Others might not be the best fit for a brand's product catalog. Qualifying "leads" means weaning out all these non-candidates from the pool of "leads" that have been gathered.

Whether a prospective customer qualifies will only be revealed through interaction and conversation with them. Having identified qualified prospects, sales leaders can engage them further by deepening the conversation with "leads". The ensuing conversation will address the remaining "leads"' needs, problems, and pain points. Sales leaders will ask questions to understand better "leads'" perspectives and concerns, as well as gain an understanding of their budgets, timelines, and requirements for using the product or service they're selling.

This conversation should weed out any remaining individuals who cannot be qualified. At the same time, it should increase the commitment the remaining "leads" make to buy the product being sold to them. This will bring sales leaders to the next step in the process: moving opportunities through the funnel. This is why sales leaders and teams focus more on nurturing the relationship they have formed with their "leads". They can do this by offering their "leads" personalized guidance, suggesting solutions to customers' needs and problems, or resolving objections.

The goal at this stage is to help the "leads" make informed buying decisions while supporting them through the decision-making process. Sales leaders and teams need to take their time at this stage. Otherwise, they risk making the customer feel like they have to rush, which is a sure way to deter them from making a buying decision. Granted, some "leads" will ultimately decide not to purchase a product, no matter how well a sales team or leader has done. That can happen for several reasons, and it is all right. A good sales leader knows this is not the end of things with such a customer. They know to make note of that customer's information so that they can reach out again and convince them to purchase in the future. This is why lost "leads" should always be included in automated sales campaigns. It is a good way to remind such "leads" of the brand's existence and bring them back to it in the future.

There is one last thing sales leaders must do to manage their sales funnels properly: evaluate and re-evaluate them constantly. This way, they can ensure that sales representatives are always using the proper methods to engage "leads" and that "leads" are smoothly moving through the funnel stages. They can likewise ensure that sales teams have everything they need to qualify "leads". They can supply their teams with all the resources required to move said "leads" through the funnel, too.

Naturally, sales leaders will face many challenges when managing their sales funnels. For instance, they might find it hard to personalize the process with "leads" while trying to reach as many people as possible. It would be all too easy for sales leaders to focus on numbers and forget to nurture the relationships they forge. Similarly, spending too much time nurturing a specific relationship with one customer at the cost of others would be easy. This is something sales leaders must always keep in the back of their minds to prevent potential hurdles.

Another challenge for sales leaders is the difficulty of distinguishing between qualified and unqualified "leads". Studies show that 62% of all "leads" are sent through the funnel, but only 27% are qualified. So, this is a more common problem in sales than you would think (Adobe Experience Cloud Team, 2018). Sales leaders can overcome this hurdle by evaluating "leads" constantly and asking themselves specific questions, like

- What would the ideal lead look like, and why?

- Why have some of our "leads" been disqualified to date?

Such questions can help leaders better understand what qualifies and disqualifies "leads", thereby showing them what to focus on throughout the process.

Customer Relationship Management And Sales Automation

Nurturing relationships is a vital part of sales funnels. Given its importance, it should not be surprising to hear that customer relationship management (CRM) is an equally vital part of a sales leader's job. CRM refers to the general practices that sales leaders adopt and the guidelines their sales teams follow when interacting with customers. These guidelines are meant to build trust between "leads" and salespeople, ultimately helping to convert the former into loyal, happy, and hopefully lifelong customers.

When focusing on CRM, sales leaders must consider a broad spectrum of communication channels. In-person conversations between sales representatives and customers are one form of communication. However, so are social media exchanges, emails, and phone calls, since there is such a thing as written communication. All the contact methods are used to create positive customer experiences and keep them returning for more (Hargrave, 2023).

These days, thanks to new technological developments like AI, sales CRM often involves various software programs. Sales leaders can use CRM technologies to quickly identify new "leads", build great customer experiences, and discover new cross-selling and upselling opportunities they might have overlooked. These benefits are recognized by most leading brands, which is why 60% of all sales leaders rely on CRM technologies to nurture their relationships with their customers (SugarCRM, 2023).

Sales leaders can use many different software programs for this, but the key piece of technology they all use is artificial intelligence (AI). About 80% of all sales leaders use AI to maximize the capabilities of their CRM programs (SugarCRM, 2023). This is because AI can rapidly analyze massive amounts of data and arrive at invaluable insights that sales representatives can use to enhance their conversations with customers and predict customer behaviors. All this fuels sales teams' abilities to do their jobs better and build trusting, positive relationships with "leads", ultimately turning them into long-term customers.

Automation is another key piece of technology that sales leaders often use. AI, once again, comes in handy for this as it is good at automating mundane or routine tasks. Say that your sales team needs to reach out to more customers, and they have decided to email a whole host of them. Doing this themselves will take quite a long time and prove draining for them (Hashemi-Pour, 2020). Having AI take care of this matter, on the other hand, will take no time at all. AI programs can mass email hundreds of potential "leads" without any issues, bringing them to your doorstep with little effort and freeing up your team's valuable time to spend on something more worthwhile.

CRM can help automate many different aspects of a sales team's job. For example, it can automate their marketing efforts by removing the various repetitive tasks that are part of it. It can automate the customer contact center, too, using chatbots and other similar technologies. At the same time, it can offer sales teams location-based services by creating marketing campaigns that are specific to certain geographic locations. This can help sales teams reach qualified "leads" quicker, significantly speeding up the process of contacting them.

CRM and automation technologies can lighten sales teams' workloads. Additionally, these technologies can quickly analyze the data obtained from prospective "leads" and existing customers. Sales leaders can use this data to craft more targeted marketing campaigns and strategies. Meanwhile, these technologies can keep track of "leads" as they move through sales funnels, making funnel management easier.

These technologies are essential because sales leaders build trust with their customers and foster deeper relationships. Studies show that only 2% of sales occur at the first meeting with a customer (Trent, 2022). Building trust through CRM matters because it leads to greater interaction and more long-term relationships. High-performing sales teams know this, so 50% of them report that their sales processes are highly monitored and automated (Weaver, 2023).

As for how much the sales process can be automated, studies indicate that more than 30% of all sales activities can be automated (Bangia et al., 2020). The benefits of automating all these processes would be monumental, seeing as they would result in things like

- increasing the sales department's productivity and efficiency.
- increasing overall sales.
- increasing customer retention long-term.
- improving lead generation at all times.
- providing customers with a better, more positive experience.

Forecast And Planning

A final tactic sales leaders can employ to optimize sales processes is forecasting and planning. Forecasting and planning are the methods sales leaders use to analyze their sales team's past and present performance to identify current trends and use them to make predictions about future trends and the team's future performance. The process can be defined as their ability to make plans based on these predictions.

Making accurate predictions is not as difficult as you might think, at least not so long as you have the correct data and insights. Obtaining the correct data can seem arduous, but the process can be made much easier and faster with the help of AI. Afterward, proper data analysis can help sales leaders draw the right conclusions and gain the necessary insights. How can you be sure you are drawing the right conclusions and insights? The trick here is to ask the right questions, like

- Who are our prospective customers? Are they decision-makers or influencers?
- What solutions do we mean to sell our "leads"? Are these solutions based on need?
- Is our company in a prime position to solve prospects' problems through its products or services? Would prospects consider purchasing this product or service? How would they benefit?
- Are there current circumstances, such as new industry regulations, that might compel prospects to purchase soon?
- Where are prospects physically making their purchase decisions? Can the sales teams be on the ground in these locations?
- How do our prospects make their purchasing decisions?

Such questions must be asked to ensure that past and present circumstances are understood accurately and thoroughly. That knowledge makes it possible for sales leaders to make accurate predictions for the future. To augment this knowledge and, thus, their capability to make accurate predictions and plans, sales leaders can also

- assess past and present historical trends to see what future ones may look like.
- adopt emerging technologies and integrate them into their sales processes early on.
- make guesses about future trends based on current market trends and their trajectories.
- observe their competitors and how they behave, analyze what this means for the future, and adapt their behavior accordingly.

When planning and forecasting, a sales leader must document everything. They must endeavor to break down their forecasts into smaller steps and individual items. That way, they will make it easier to follow and understand, as well as form plans based on their forecast.

CHAPTER 6

SALES TECHNIQUES AND TRAINING

———————◆———————

Honest and transparent content is the best sales tool in the world. Period.

–Marcus Sheridan

If a sales team were a ship, a sales leader could be considered its captain. As captains of their ships, sales leaders oversee their crews, meaning their sales teams. That responsibility extends to training them to be the best sales representatives. After all, the successes of sales representatives and teams are the successes of sales leaders. Now, as you are aware, there are several sales strategies that leaders can opt for.

Similarly, there are many sales techniques and methodologies to choose from. These are techniques and methodologies that sales leaders must be familiar with and train their sales teams in. So, which methodologies should sales leaders opt for?

The answer to that question usually depends on the kind of sales strategy they have gone with. Still, specific methodologies often prove more effective than others. Knowing which ones and how they work can help sales leaders decide their strategies. It will make it easier for sales leaders to train their teams in those methodologies if they are knowledgeable about them. No one wants to learn from a teacher who does not know what subject they are teaching.

Sales Methodologies

A *sales methodology* can be defined as the framework or principles that salespeople use to convince and close the customer they are talking to. They are the easy-to-execute set of steps salespeople must take to meet their sales goals. Since specific methodologies have proven highly effective, they can be considered "best practices," in a sense. With that in mind, the best practices sales leaders could train their salespeople in are:

- Situation, problem, implication, and need (SPIN) selling
- Need, economic impact, access to authority, and time (NEAT) selling
- Simplicity, being invaluable, alignment, and raising priorities (SNAP) selling
- Challenger selling
- Solution Selling

To start, SPIN selling is a methodology that starts with the sales leader defining the situation by asking, "What product is the customer currently using?" Again, they identify the problem by asking, "What need is that product not meeting?" They then move on to implications, as in what having this problem implies for the customer (Frost, 2021). That might mean anything from a loss of productivity and efficiency to disrupted focus or something entirely different. Finally, they define the need payoff, which explains what solution would be better than the one the customer is currently using and why.

This is how the SPIN methodology presents offers to new customers. The steps the sales process follows, though, are a little different:

1. The salesperson contacts a prospective customer and

investigates how their product could help them. This is where the situation, problem, and implication aspects of SPIN selling come in.

2. They demonstrate how and why their solution works by showing its benefits, advantages, and various features.

3. They anticipate prospective customers' objections and prepare their responses for them.

SPIN selling is like NEAT selling in that needs are a significant part, yet the two differ in key aspects. NEAT selling is a methodology where the key is to anticipate customer needs (Lucid Content Team, 2019). This is followed by helping the customer grasp the economic impact the solution will have. In other words, the next step of the process is to explain the value of the product on offer. That is followed up with access to authority, which identifies who can put the seller in touch with those in charge of making buying decisions for an organization. The last step of the methodology is qualifying the timeline and creating implications for meeting it.

So, NEAT selling starts with salespeople asking what the customer needs and putting themselves in the customer's shoes to figure it out. Empathy is a crucial part of this step, but not necessarily the next one, which is the economic impact. This stage weighs the economic impact of the current solution that a customer is using against the economic impact of the one offered. In other words, it evaluates the value difference between the two solutions. When that is done, the process moves onto stage three, where salespeople figure out who has the decision-making capabilities in an account. To that end, they practice account mapping, a way to visualize the different individuals in a customer organization and their relationship dynamics, to figure out how to reach the right person in an organization (Gangoli, 2022). They finalize everything with the last step, clarifying the best timeline for getting a deal and working within the parameters of this knowledge.

NEAT selling is like SNAP selling in that both methodologies take time into account in different ways. NEAT selling determines the best time to try to sell something to someone. SNAP selling specifically targets busy customers who are overwhelmed by all their responsibilities and priorities. The methodology it employs makes such buyers pause what they are doing and take an interest in what is being said to them. In other words, it makes them more attentive to what a salesperson has to say. That can be challenging, especially when customers feel frazzled and have many distractions. Luckily, SNAP selling was explicitly developed for such customers.

How about SNAP selling? As you will recall, the "S" in SNAP selling is simplicity. Simplicity means keeping things simple and easy to explain. It also means tailoring pitches to customers' specific needs. Being iNvaluable is about the salesperson proving their trustworthiness to the customer and laying out all the benefits they stand to gain by purchasing a product or service. Alignment means focusing on customer concerns, anticipating them, and addressing them quickly. It also means understanding customer goals and ensuring the solutions can help customers meet them. Finally, raising priorities means linking product services to the customers' priorities, which may otherwise prove distracting.

Doing all this necessitates a deep understanding of customers. For this, salespeople must first identify decision-makers. Then, they must use a buyer's matrix to list and anticipate the kinds of questions customers may ask and answer them in advance. Building customer personas is naturally a part of this process, too, as it grants further insights into the people sales teams are targeting. Of course, sales teams must empathize with these customers and put themselves in their shoes. That way, they will be able to understand customers all the better and make pitches to them that are truly wanted.

Then there is the challenger method, which seems to be on the rise lately. Studies show that 40% of all high-performing salespeople use this method to close deals (Mares, 2023). The **challenger method** is simple in theory: salespeople offer customers a new perspective and do not shy away from challenging conversations about costs, which are all too familiar. For this method to work, salespeople must understand the leverage they hold and the value they offer their customers. They must identify the customer's specific problems or needs. They must then tailor their pitch to address those problems or needs tactfully.

The great thing about the Challenger method is that it pairs well with other methodologies, such as solution selling. Solution selling prompts salespeople to consider customers, as usual, and recommend solutions that can solve their problems (Kelwig, 2024). This method is most effective for customers who have specific pain points and problems that require targeted solutions. When such problems are not explicitly targeted in the sales methodology, sales teams come across as trying to peddle something customers do not need. This is the opposite of the impression they want to give.

The first step in the solution-selling process is understanding the product that's being offered and knowing it inside and out. This is followed by salespeople qualifying their "leads" and forming customer personas to determine their needs. Having done so, sales teams outline what customers' needs are not currently being met, which they can do by incorporating some SPIN selling techniques. As problems are identified, sales teams ask how they might be solved and try to be as specific in their questions and answers as possible. They link their answers to the product or service they are trying to sell at all times. In doing so, they highlight its value and develop the ability to articulate it to customers effectively. This enables them to make compelling pitches and close sales successfully.

One thing you may have noticed about these methodologies is that they always include a research phase. This is because understanding customers and their needs is a key part of these methodologies' processes. This is also a key part of the process involved in choosing a sales methodology. Only by gaining a clear understanding of their customers can sales leaders determine the most effective sales approach. Choosing the proper methodology starts with mapping the sales process, step by step, after thorough research. This clarity reveals which approaches align best with the existing process and the product or service offered (Brudner, 2022), enabling the sales leader to make an informed choice. Once decided, they can cascade the strategy to their teams and train them on the methodologies, a rollout that demands exceptional communication skills. Sales leaders will communicate their chosen methodologies to sales teams in two ways: through the training materials they prepare and by speaking with them directly. If there is one skill sales leaders need to master to ensure their methodology is understood correctly, it is their communication skills, whether written or oral. Poor communication skills guarantee that the methods a sales leader tries to train their team in will be misunderstood and mishandled.

Communication Skills

There are certain specific communication skills sales leaders can pick up to ensure this does not happen. The first such skill is active listening, which we have touched on before. Active listening is important because it allows sales leaders to hear the objections salespeople may raise to the methodologies they lay out for them (O'Bryan, 2022). Thus, it enables them to address those objections and convince everyone that the chosen methodology is the best strategy. Active listening further enables sales leaders to identify problems before they escalate into significant issues and solve them quickly and efficiently. It helps them connect with their sales representatives and build trusting relationships with them, too.

Empathy is another vital tool for communication. Empathy helps salespeople understand their customers and their needs properly, thus enabling them to meet their needs. It does the same thing for sales leaders regarding their team members. It enables leaders to put themselves in team members' place and quickly spot situations in which they might raise objections, misunderstand instructions, or face challenges (Indeed Editorial Team, 2023c). This further enables them to put the objections to rest, solve misunderstandings, and offer solutions to team members' challenges. All in all, empathy can increase team members' understanding of the methodologies presented to them and decrease their resistance to learning them.

One of the most effective ways sales leaders can develop empathy is by practicing curiosity. Curiosity is a powerful communication tool, it enhances emotional intelligence and self-awareness, both of which are essential for showing genuine empathy (Roberts, 2023). Moreover, it helps you keep an open mind, making you more approachable and allowing you to notice and use emerging trends and technologies more rapidly. It enables you to learn and develop new skills, improving your problem-solving and creativity. In addition to all that, curiosity helps you build better relationships. A sales leader who openly practices curiosity builds stronger relationships with their team members. This inevitably improves communication between sales leaders and their teams. It does away with some of the hesitancy that team members may feel when approaching their sales leaders with questions and concerns. It allows for a relaxed environment where open and honest communication can always be pursued, just as it should be.

Open and honest communication is a good policy for sales leaders to adopt, regardless of whether they communicate with team members, "leads", or established customers. It is a vital policy for customers because it establishes long-term credibility and builds trust. These two things often translate to long-term, if not life-long, customer loyalty. Therefore, sales leaders need always to be open and honest with "leads" and customers, encouraging their team members to do the same. Team members should never lie to customers or exaggerate the facts. Customers can usually sense dishonesty, and when they do, they are likely to walk away. Worse still, they may share their negative experience with others, damaging the brand's reputation in the process. A brand is only as good as its reputation, so that is the last thing any sales leader ever wants.

There are additional benefits to pursuing an open and honest communication policy. It makes the sales process transparent (*7 Reasons Why Honesty*, 2019). That is good because transparency builds trust, helps team members identify and address customer concerns effectively, and typically leads to more sales. It also helps set customers' expectations accurately, ensuring that they will not be disappointed later and that they, therefore, will not renege on a buying decision. Openness and honesty, then, help customers prevent buyer's remorse. On the sales team's side, adopting a policy of openness and honesty makes sales leaders more approachable, relatable, and far easier to talk to. Thus, it proves to be the second-best policy sales leaders can ever adopt.

As for what the best communication policy for sales leaders is, that honor falls to their decision to communicate with their team members in a concise, clear, simple, but concrete manner. Being concise is important because rambling, whether in conversation or writing, is a sure way to confuse people. When you ramble, you drown people in information, making it hard for them to pinpoint the essential instructions they need to follow. Such things lead to misunderstandings, mistakes, delays, and mismanagement of accounts, which can result in their loss.

The same can be said for overly complicated instructions and explanations, highlighting the importance of keeping things simple. As for what being concrete means when communicating with sales teams, sales leaders would use examples and case studies, especially when discussing the methodologies they expect them to use. Examples and case studies can clearly illustrate what sales leaders want done, leaving no room for confusion about what team members are expected to do. This clarity will make it infinitely easier for them to do their jobs well, thereby carrying their sales teams to new heights.

Handling Objections

We have mentioned how proper communication can help sales leaders handle objections previously. Objections are important to focus on because, no matter how effective a sales methodology is, customers can come up with all sorts of reasons why they cannot purchase a specific product. Anticipating such objections is part of a sales leader's job, as is coming up with practical ways to counter them. Doing thorough research into customers by building customer personas will help sales leaders understand specific kinds of customers on an intimate level. Thus, it will help them identify pain points that are exclusive to them. Having identified those, sales leaders can start generating counterarguments and solutions.

There are some specific objections that all customers might raise. The most common of these objections involves a lack of

- resources
- urgency
- trust
- need (Ye, 2022)

If a customer lacks resources, they believe they lack the necessary budget to purchase the product or service being offered to them. This is the objection salespeople will come across most often. Knowing this, they will have to find a way to convince customers otherwise. The most effective way of doing this is to demonstrate that the product they are trying to sell is valuable enough to justify the expense. They can do this by asking, "What reward does this product offer that makes it worth the risk?" or a similar question. Whatever answers salespeople come up with are the counterarguments they will present to their customers when this objection arises.

When a customer lacks urgency, it means they do not believe they need the product right now. They may have a problem, but they do not see it as pressing. To overcome this, salespeople must reframe the issue, showing why it is more urgent than the customer realizes. Start by asking why they do not view the problem as important. Then, use active listening to uncover the excuses behind their hesitation and the genuine concerns those excuses hide. With those insights, craft a targeted, compelling argument that dismantles the objection and moves the conversation forward.

Another common objection is a lack of trust, something that often arises when a prospective customer is engaging with a brand for the first time and has no prior experience with it. The only effective way to overcome this is by building a relationship, educating the prospect about the brand, and earning their trust over time. It is a gradual process, which is why salespeople must take a long-term approach, grounded in transparency, consistency, and honesty.

The final common objection salespeople may encounter is a lack of need. This objection means that the customer fails to see how the offered product will solve their issue or meet a specific need. Facing this objection is an excellent opportunity for salespeople because it allows them to explain and demonstrate why their product can help the customer. It allows them to ask open-ended questions that help them better understand their customers' pain points and needs. Having obtained this information, they will be able to tailor their pitch to the specific needs of the customer, convincingly showing them that they need the product they are looking at.

Closing Techniques

A good sales leader knows the kinds of objections their team members may encounter and prepares them to face them. They also know that they must teach their sales teams effective closing techniques, given the several techniques available to salespeople. Again, good sales leaders know that some of these techniques are more effective than others, and the most effective among them are:

- question closing
- summary closing
- soft angle closing
- unique offer closing
- the alternative close (Turkington, 2023)

Of these, **question closing** involves asking probing questions to prospects throughout the conversation to address objections and encourage a purchase. Some examples of questions used in this technique might be:

- Does the product I described sound like it could help resolve your current issue?
- Is there a specific reason why we cannot proceed with the deal?
- What needs do you think this service fails to meet?

Such questions allow salespeople to identify, and address missed concerns or ask for closure, often leading to a sale.

This technique differs from a **summary closing**, which involves summarizing the discussion and highlighting key points. This closing is a good way to remind customers of the benefits they can expect and the needs they can meet by purchasing a product. It is a good way of encouraging the customer to purchase without being overbearing.

Then there is the **soft angle closing**, which similarly

allows salespeople to go over the benefits of their products but then has them follow it up with a low-impact question. A low-impact question gauges whether a prospective customer is open to hearing more about a product. "Would you like to hear more?" is an excellent, though obvious, example of what such a question may look like.

Meanwhile, the **unique offer closing** is an excellent tactic for large deals, and it can come in handy when the prospective customer gets cold feet. The technique revolves around offering the customer a unique offer, be it a trial period, a special discount, or something else, when they start to hesitate. The offer is presented and followed by a question such as, *'Would that interest you?'* Framing the offer this way encourages greater customer engagement and interest. Of course, they would have to get permission from their manager or sales leaders to make such an offer. So long as they do that, the technique can prove incredibly effective and result in large sales deals.

As for the **alternative close**, this method involves presenting customers with multiple buying options. Human beings like having a sense of control and often become more likely to make a buying decision when presented with choices, as it makes them feel they are in control of the transaction. For example, offering premium and basic plans is one way of doing this. The technique is particularly effective because, when used, the customer's decision often turns from "Should I buy or not?" to "Which version of the product should I buy?"

CHAPTER 7
CUSTOMER-CENTRIC SELLING

———————◆———————

If you are not taking care of your customer, your competitor will

–Bob Hooey

You have probably heard the old saying, "The customer is always right." Now, this is not always true. If a customer walks into a vegan restaurant and then demands to talk to the manager upon realizing there is no meat on the menu, you would be hard-pressed to claim that customer was "right." The saying, however, can often prove to be true for sales departments. As such, it is a notion for sales leaders to keep in mind if they are to understand customer needs and preferences and make tailored pitches to them that can meet those needs and preferences.

There are many strategies, methodologies, and techniques that sales leaders can master and train their departments in, as you have seen. One commonality they all share is that they are exceptionally customer-centric. The focus is always on the customer's needs, problems, and wants. That is just as it should be, because sales teams and leaders need to adopt a customer-centric approach to succeed. Thus, they must remember that "the customer is always right" and act accordingly.

Understanding Customer Needs

Practicing customer-centric selling requires understanding

customer needs first and foremost. As you have seen, this process begins with building a customer profile, but it does not end there. There are many things sales leaders and teams can do to better understand their customers. You are already familiar with some of these techniques, like empathy. Fostering empathy for the customer is essential to the sales process, making it easier to put the customer's needs first. This works best when sales leaders practice situational empathy. Situational empathy is an individual's empathetic response to a situation that has been triggered. A salesperson who practices situational empathy observes a problem that a customer is having and immediately responds to it with empathy. It is as simple as that.

Situational empathy is just as effective a sales technique as a simple one because it allows salespeople to grasp their customers' needs and respond honestly and promptly. A great example of how this works can be seen in Help Scout's Whole Company Support system. The Whole Company Support system expects every sales team member, from those at the lowest rungs to the sales leaders, to understand and focus on customers' stories. It expects them to use those stories to understand customers' needs and then use that information to improve their job performance and enhance the product they sell.

Help Scout's Whole Company Support system essentially uses customer feedback to accomplish all this. It does so because studies show that for every customer who complains about something, 26 others are experiencing the same problem but not saying anything about it (Ciotti, 2023). So, Help Scout recognizes that by helping one customer, they can help many more. Hence, they focus on customer feedback, both positive and negative, at all times and use it to create better products that can appeal to more customers and turn them into lifelong brand ambassadors.

Customer feedback can be invaluable, a tool that you will learn how to use later on in this chapter, particularly in the context of a customer-centric approach. It pairs particularly well with another invaluable tool in a sales leader's arsenal: curiosity. You already know that curiosity is a tool that can improve a sales leader's communication skills. That, however, is not all that it is capable of. Studies show that 82% of the top salespeople in the country have incredibly high levels of curiosity (Martin, 2011). This is because curiosity prompts question-asking. Sales leaders and teams need to be able to ask the right questions of their customers to understand and meet their needs appropriately.

A sales leader cannot even figure out the right question to ask a customer if they do not practice curiosity, let alone actually ask it. Likewise, they cannot bring themselves to ask questions if they do not maintain an open and honest dialogue with their customers. Maintaining an open and honest dialogue is a pillar of customer-centric selling, as is the willingness to walk away instead of persistently pushing a product on a customer when you know it is not the best fit for them. While pushing a product on a customer who does not need it may result in a sale, it will also result in buyer's remorse. That will prevent the buyer from becoming a repeat customer. It will also make them more likely to talk to others about how ineffective the product was, thereby damaging the brand's reputation.

There are two questions a salesperson has to ask if they want to avoid pushing products on customers who neither need nor want them:

1. If the person I am selling to agrees to buy this product, will their life improve?

2. When my interaction with this customer is over, will the world be better than when it began?

If the answer to those questions is "no," then the salesperson will "push" a product to the customer by persisting in their efforts to sell. Upon realizing this, a good sales leader's advice would be simple: Thank the customer for their time, let them walk away, and move on to the next one.

Consultative Selling

We have covered several selling strategies so far, but there is one highly customer-centric approach that we have not tried: consultative selling. It is a bit of a shame, considering how effective consultative selling is as a strategy, and thus, it merits some attention of its own. Consultative selling focuses on customer needs and earns their trust and loyalty before offering a solution. Like all the strategies we have covered so far, consultative selling is based on certain tenets, these being:

- balancing insights with questions
- building trust through knowledge
- owning the conversation
- having genuine conversations
- letting feedback and research be your guide
- active listening (Taylor, 2023)

The first of these tenets, balancing insights with questions, is born from the desire to understand customers' needs. Since developing an understanding necessitates asking the right questions, this strategy involves asking many questions. This approach highlights the importance of asking clarifying questions while offering meaningful insights throughout the conversation. Without this balance, the dialogue can start to feel more like an interrogation—

something that can easily turn customers off.

One effective way to maintain engagement is by responding to a customer's answer with an observation about their challenge and explaining how the product can help address it. This technique also supports another key principle: building trust through knowledge.

Trust is not built overnight or in a single conversation—seasoned sales professionals know this well. That is why they prioritize follow-up calls and meetings. During these follow-ups, they revisit previous discussions, reinforce key points, express appreciation for the customer's time, and invite further questions or concerns. These consistent touchpoints not only provide valuable information but also reinforce the salesperson's reliability, and, by extension, the credibility of the brand they represent.

Similar results can be achieved when salespeople take ownership of their conversations. This is a core element of the consultative selling approach, where the salesperson acts as a trusted advisor or guide. Like any good guide, they are knowledgeable, confident, and clear about the path forward.

To earn that level of trust, salespeople must demonstrate credibility by confidently leading the conversation. This does not mean dominating the discussion or talking over the customer; instead, it is essential to create space for the customer to share their thoughts and ask questions. However, it does mean maintaining direction and control, guiding the dialogue with purpose and clarity.

The next tenet, having genuine conversations, is important for further establishing trust and reliability and showing customers that you care about them and their needs. Consider what a genuine conversation typically looks like. Someone having such a conversation would probably be quite empathetic and enthusiastic as they speak. They would say they mean every word they say and are not just talking for the sake of it. Salespeople need to evoke this kind of sense as they talk to prospective customers. That is why honesty and transparency are essential. A salesperson who does not genuinely believe in the product they are offering will struggle to succeed, because they will not come across as authentic or credible to the customer.

Salespeople going with the consultative strategy must always let customer feedback act as their guide. This goes for both positive and negative feedback, as it can give salespeople a sense of what to maintain and what to avoid. They can develop a better sense of these things if they take notes based on the feedback they receive. They may find those notes especially helpful if they lead them to new solutions for meeting customer needs, ultimately helping them close new deals.

The final tenet of consultative selling is active listening, a massively useful tool, as you know. Actively and intentionally listening to customers requires allowing them to voice their thoughts, concerns, and observations. It means not interrupting them as they talk and paying attention to the meaning behind their words and their nonverbal cues, like facial expressions. It even means empathizing with customers, which brings us right back to our first tenet, thereby getting them to understand that their concerns and needs matter to you, an approach that often earns that person's trust and leads to them becoming a lifelong customer.

Building Long-Term Relationships

As you might have noticed, the customer-centric approach in general and consultative selling emphasize the importance of building long-term relationships with customers. They do so because that earns a customer's loyalty and ensures customer retention. It creates brand loyalty, translating to steady sales for years and brand ambassadors freely advertising the brand in question (Talbot, 2021).

Brand loyalty is something that all sales leaders and their teams want to inspire in their customers. This is partly because brand loyalty strengthens the sales funnel of a brand, which is of great interest to sales leaders. It also lowers marketing costs for a brand since those customers become brand ambassadors, which helps spread the word about its products at no cost. Inspiring brand loyalty, though, is not just about selling people products they like. At its core, it is about adding value to people's lives (Wilkinson, 2023).

Think about it this way, would you go back to a restaurant if the food was bland? Probably not. However, what if the food was excellent, like, best-meal-of-your-life amazing? You would not just return; you would probably bring your friends, rave about it to your family, and tell anyone who would listen. You would become a walking, talking ad for that place. Why?

Because the experience gave you real value, and that kind of value naturally turns people into brand ambassadors.

To inspire brand loyalty, sales leaders and teams must consistently pay attention to their customers. In other words, they have to check in on them regularly to ensure their needs and expectations are being met. It means exceeding their expectations consistently. It even means doing things like

- keeping track of customer demands and creating a

realistic timeline to meet them.

- offering reasonable and healthy incentives to customers like discounts or promo codes in exchange for referrals, social media shares, and other means of getting the word out there.

- always maintaining a positive attitude when interacting with customers and prospects in terms of words, tone of voice, and attitude.

- always prioritizing customer experience, regardless of what sales strategy has been adopted.

- regularly going over the customer feedback that you have, drawing useful insights from it, and using them to improve the product on offer, as well as the customer experience itself (Wilkinson, 2023).

Customer Feedback

Throughout this chapter, you have consistently come across two key words: customer feedback. Customer feedback is one of the most important tools any sales leader or team can use. This is because customer feedback comes from customer experience. According to one study, 93% of customers are more likely to repeat purchases at a brand if customer service has been excellent in their experience (Redbord, 2023). There is a mountain of data and evidence to back up this fact. For example, customers are 2.6 times more likely to purchase from a brand again if they have had a positive experience with them. Another is that positive customer experiences increase profits by 25–95% while increasing customer retention by 5% (Redbord, 2023).

So, customer feedback is the key to providing customers with a positive experience and thus reaping these benefits. Customer feedback is not confined to the comments emailed to you by satisfied or unsatisfied customers. There are multiple channels through which sales leaders can gather feedback. The primary channels they can turn to for this are (HubSpot, n.d.):

- product-services feedback
- customer service feedback
- sales feedback

Product-service feedback is the comments from customers about your product or services. Product-service feedback can take many forms. It might have to do, for instance, with bugs or production errors. It might be about new features customers would like to see in that product. Customers might be concerned about areas for improvement in the product or aspects that are doing well. In any case, product service feedback can be used to fix issues in the product and improve it in various ways. Thus, the products or services on offer can be improved, appeal to a broader customer base in the long run, and satisfy the customers who initially shared their comments with the brand's sales department.

Customer service feedback concerns customers' general experience with the product or service they have bought. It may also have to do with what kind of experience, good, bad, or something in between, they have with the company's customer service team. Customer service feedback can be relayed to sales teams through live chats, reviews, email follow-ups, and other channels. Once a sales team gets this feedback, they can start analyzing it. This enables them to pinpoint areas for improvement or issues with the customer experience. They can then start brainstorming on how these problems can be solved and improvements can be made to enhance the customers' experience.

Finally, there is sales and marketing feedback, which may address unmet customer expectations, particularly if said expectations were set in either sales meetings by the sales team or through marketing campaigns. Regardless of where these expectations were set, receiving sales or marketing feedback typically means dealing with angry or upset customers. So, the first order of business here will be to calm the customers down and understand why their expectations were not met. Perhaps the reason for this is a misunderstanding in the sales process about the product's intended purpose. It could be due to a technical setback where the promised upgrade was delayed, or there might be something entirely different going on.

Whatever the case, sales teams must first understand what is wrong and then focus on fixing it. They must identify what needs to change in the sales and marketing processes to prevent similar misunderstandings or mishaps from happening again. They must then take the necessary steps to ensure this remains the case. Doing so will require adhering to the customer feedback loop (Jangra, 2023). This simple loop begins when a sales leader asks for customer feedback. Upon receiving it, they categorize it, meaning they determine the type of feedback so it can be relayed to the right person. If feedback concerns a technical bug, it must be relayed to the IT team ASAP, for instance.

Once feedback has been categorized, a decision must be made on how to respond. What changes will need to be made in response to the feedback? How urgently do those changes need to take place? What is the realistic time frame in which they can take place? Once the answers to these questions are determined, sales leaders can take action to correct the issue, manage expectations, improve customer service experience, or implement any other measures.

Once action has been taken, the next step in the loop is to check in with the customers and ask for their thoughts. In other words, it is to ask for feedback on how the situation was handled and see whether things have been resolved to their satisfaction. This will start the feedback loop all over again. Of course, all the while, new feedback from new customers will be coming in, thus keeping the loop going indefinitely.

CHAPTER 8

SALES TECHNOLOGY AND TRENDS

———————◆———————

At least 40% of all businesses will die in the next 10 years...
If they don't figure out how to change their entire company
to accommodate new technologies.

–John Chambers

I f you are a millennial, you belong to a generation that
has witnessed firsthand the dramatic changes the world
can undergo in a single lifetime, primarily driven by the
rapid advancement of technology. When millennials were
kids, computers were either not around or they were
hulking machines that not everyone got to have. Connecting
to the internet was an ordeal that required no one to use the
landline. Cell phones came with a million buttons, meaning
touchscreens were not a thing, at least outside of sci-fi
movies. All this changed in just a few years. Most
millennials found that they were living in a completely
different world by their teens and twenties. Now, everyone
has a laptop and a tablet at home. Internet connectivity is
superfast and has nothing to do with landlines, especially
since landlines have nearly gone extinct. Meanwhile,
smartphones, with their touchscreens and millions of apps,
are in everyone's hands.

These technological changes that millennials grew up
experiencing and that became a part of everyone's lives
changed the business world when you think about it. This is
all thanks to the development of new technologies and their

corresponding marketing strategies, like websites, emails, subscription services, and social media marketing. Things are still in the process of changing, thanks to the advent of newer technologies like AI. These technologies will continue to transform various aspects of the business world. Sales departments are no exception to this. Consequently, new technologies will impact the responsibilities of sales teams and leaders. Effective sales leaders are all too aware of this. Hence, they make a point of staying current. They try to adopt new technologies as they arise and use them well. At the same time, they strive to remain open-minded regarding emerging developments.

Sales Analytics And Big Data

Sales leaders have many important responsibilities; staying current on new technologies and incorporating them into their sales teams is one of them. This responsibility might not seem like a big deal initially, but it is more vital to sales leaders than you would think. This is due to a couple of key reasons. The first is that many of the emerging technologies we are currently witnessing can increase the amount of data we access and the insights we can draw from them. Take AI, for instance. Currently, AI programs can sort through and analyze mountains of customer data. They can then draw a host of conclusions from that data, and sales leaders can use those conclusions to find new ways of solving problems, meeting needs, using emerging market trends, and reaching new customers. The data and insights that new technologies give access to are vital for sales leaders and can make them and their teams infinitely better at their jobs.

This is just one reason why technology is important for sales leaders. Another is that emerging technologies significantly automate the tedious, repetitive, administrative, and monotonous tasks that sales teams and leaders would otherwise have to handle. This frees up significant time for those teams and leaders and keeps them from wasting their energy needlessly. That is time and energy they can use to do more productive things, like qualifying more "leads", coming up with new sales strategies, and closing more deals.

Still, despite these reasons, some people might hesitate to adopt new technologies. We human beings like the things we are used to, after all, and approach change with some skepticism, even when we know that such changes can and will benefit us. Suppose a sales leader is hesitant to consider new technologies for their sales teams. In that case, they must remind themselves of the third reason why adopting new technologies is important: The rest of the industry will inevitably adopt those technologies. If those sales leaders do not follow suit, they will be left behind by their competitors, unable to keep up with them. Over time, they will become irrelevant and forgotten, much like MySpace, for example.

Big Data Analytics

Now that we know the many benefits technology can offer sales leaders, let us take a closer look at them. One of the benefits of technology is that it helps with data collection and analysis. Data collection and analysis are key responsibilities of sales leaders. This task is made infinitely easier by technology, which can collect, synthesize, and analyze oceans of data faster than any human being ever could. The technology that can do this is officially referred to as data analytics. Big data analytics analyzes large and complex data sets, extracting insights from them. Sales leaders then use those insights to make pertinent strategic decisions. As of the writing of this book, the technologies that are available to sales leaders for this end are:

- Machine learning, which is AI's ability to study statistical algorithms to learn from the data it is presented with
- Data mining, which is the technology's ability to sort through large data sets and discover patterns within them
- Natural language processing, which applies computational tactics to natural human language when interacting with human customers, thereby drawing valuable insights from what those customers are saying

Tools such as these can uncover patterns, relationships, and trends within the data they are given. Sales leaders can utilize this information to develop innovative sales and marketing strategies for their teams. They can also use this information to find new ways of meeting emerging customers' needs and wants, thereby becoming capable of meeting them before anyone else and getting ahead of market trends (Chatterjee et al., 2022). A great example of this can be seen at Amazon. Amazon uses big data analytics to analyze customers' browsing and purchase histories. Based on that analysis, the website recommends personalized products to its customers. Since those recommendations usually align with what the customers are looking for and their needs, it often results in them making new purchases. Thus, the system Amazon has put in place actively drives sales and generates revenue.

Big data analytics isn't just suitable for driving sales, though. It can be great for other things, too, like

- optimizing operations, such as supply chain management, by identifying ongoing patterns to identify emerging trends and future problems, like one that can disrupt the supply chain.

- providing customers with a more positive and satisfactory experience by using data to identify their preferences, thereby helping sales leaders and teams create more personalized offers for them.
- streamlining processes by removing various tasks from sales leaders' and teams' plates, giving them the ability to focus on more productive tasks, which ultimately leads to a revenue increase.
- designing more effective marketing campaigns by allowing sales leaders to better understand ongoing and emerging trends, along with customer preferences and needs.
- streamlining production by removing tasks from team members' plates and reducing costs by identifying more efficient alternatives and areas of waste.
- supporting more informed decision-making processes across the board (*How Big Data Analytics Helps*, 2023).

Sales In The Digital Age

An added benefit of technology is that sales leaders can use it to empower their teams. They can do this in many ways. For example, they can incorporate CRM technologies into their processes, as discussed in earlier chapters. CRM technologies are software tools that help team members manage customer tickets efficiently and keep track of ongoing or planned campaigns (Kelwig, 2022). They can help team members identify "leads" that will end in sales more quickly, saving them time. They can streamline processes such as finding and organizing customer data, generating insights from it, and building sales processes that revolve around customers.

CRM technologies can also use sales automation to help

team members track their interactions with prospects and customers, improve their sales strategies, and further personalize their communications with their contacts. All in all, CRM technologies can make work significantly easier for sales team members and improve their performance and productivity, which is precisely what sales leaders want.

CRM is not the only technology sales leaders might consider adopting to help their sales teams. Various other technologies can also be considered, like mobile technologies and, of course, artificial intelligence (Hiltbrand, 2023). *Mobile technologies* are programs that sales team members can use on their smartphones. Having such technologies on their phones can be vital for team members' ability to do their jobs well, especially since they are almost always on the go. Mobile technologies can help them access information that may be critical in their decision-making processes, such as determining how to approach a specific prospect and which sales strategy, methodology, or technique to employ when interacting with them. These technologies would also enable team members to communicate with prospects and customers anytime and anywhere, thus making them even more efficient and productive in the long run.

Then there is AI. By now, it is undeniable that AI can be of immeasurable help to sales teams. Studies show that incorporating AI into sales processes cuts costs by 40–60%, reduces call times by as much as 70%, and increases the number of "leads" and appointments that sales teams secure by 50% (Baumgartner et al., 2016). Part of the reason why AI can do all this is that it is good at data analytics, particularly sales analytics, as we have established. Another part of the reason, though, is that AI increases team members' efficiency by decreasing their workload. At the same time, it predicts customers' needs better than we mere mortals can, thus enhancing team members' ability to meet them.

Considering all this, it should not be surprising that sales experts believe that 75% of all B2B companies in the country will have incorporated AI systems into their sales processes by 2025 (Agbede, 2024). Contrary to some fears, this will not mean AI will ultimately replace sales teams. Instead, it will just mean that AI will continue to enhance teams' performance and ability to do their jobs by leaps and bounds for years to come. This goes just as much for sales leaders themselves as it does for their teams. After all, AI plays a massive role in determining ongoing and emerging market trends these days. Determining market trends is vital to any sales leader's job because it enables them to implement the most effective sales strategies, particularly in the digital space.

Studies show that 80% of sales are expected to occur in the digital sphere in the near future (Robertson, 2020). Hence, sales leaders' ability to develop the most effective digital sales strategies is more important than ever. AI will play a key role in this, but the human component, which sales leaders themselves add, should not be overlooked. As it happens, there are many things sales leaders can do to improve their digital sales strategies. Being active on social media is one of them (Fuchs, 2022). That might sound strange to some, but social media is one of our most effective marketing and sales tools. It is a great place for salespeople to operate, giving them plenty of outreach opportunities to promote content, discover new trends, and track what customers like about their brand. So, being present on social media gives leaders new information they can use to strategize.

The same can be said for working with and empowering brand ambassadors. You already know that earning brand loyalty from customers can make a true difference. This practice can be taken a step further, though. Sales leaders can encourage, empower, and support the brand ambassadors whose loyalty they have earned. They can do so by posting their comments and testimonials online (with their permission). Social media can be great for this. A sales leader's brand website can also work. Sharing satisfied customers' comments can amplify a brand's positive reputation and serve as a great digital marketing tool.

One last thing sales leaders can do to enhance their digital marketing efforts is publish case studies and original content. This is where content marketing comes into the picture once more. Such innovative, positive content can amplify a brand's messages. It can enhance their reputation among people and attract new prospects. These prospects can then come to the brand themselves, and sales teams can convert them into lifelong customers.

FINAL THOUGHTS

B eing a successful sales leader is not just a role, it is a responsibility that shapes the future of your team, your customers, and your organization. Throughout *The Strategic Sales Leader: Architecting Vision, Driving Growth*, we have seen that sales leadership goes far beyond managing numbers or processes. It is about crafting a vision, setting the tone, and inspiring a group of individuals to perform at levels they did not think possible.

Great sales leaders are part strategist, part coach, part motivator, and part visionary. They anticipate challenges, seize opportunities, and cultivate trust both inside and outside their teams. They build processes that work, cultures that thrive, and relationships that last.

Having said that, knowledge is only potential power. The strategies, tools, and insights in this book are the foundation. What turns them into results is **consistent, deliberate action**. That means committing to your vision, leading by example, and refusing to settle for mediocrity.

Your journey as a sales leader will not be without challenges. There will be objections, market changes, and moments of doubt. However, equipped with the frameworks you now possess, you can meet them head-on, not just to survive, but to lead with confidence, clarity, and control.

The next move is yours. Step forward, apply what you have learned, and make your mark, not only as a sales leader, but as the kind of leader whose influence lasts long after the deals are done.

The Sales Leader's Action Plan

(Keep this visible. Live by it. Lead by it.)

---

1 – Clarify Your Vision

☐ Define your ultimate sales goal.

☐ Identify the culture you want to build.

☐ Share your vision clearly and consistently with your team.

---

2 – Build Your A-Team

☐ Recruit people with the right skills *and* cultural fit.

☐ Align each role with the person's strengths.

☐ Train your team in the methodologies that best fit your market.

---

3 – Master Active Listening

☐ Use it to uncover customer needs and hidden objections.

☐ Apply it within your team to resolve issues early.

☐ Listen for both words *and* what is behind them.

---

4 – Create & Execute Your Sales Playbook

☐ Map out every step of your sales process.

☐ Integrate proven methodologies, adapted to your business.

☐ Ensure every team member knows and follows it.

---

5 – Measure What Matters

☐ Set relevant, trackable KPIs.

☐ Review performance data regularly.

☐ Make decisions based on evidence, not assumptions.

6 – Lead with Consistency & Energy

☐ Maintain open, transparent communication at all times.

☐ Inspire and motivate your team daily.

☐ Model the behaviour and standards you expect.

7 – Adapt & Evolve

☐ Stay ahead of market trends and shifts.

☐ Refine your strategies regularly.

☐ Encourage innovation within your team.

☑ **Review weekly** – Adjust as needed to stay on track.

☑ **Share openly** – Make sure your team understands and owns the plan.

☑ **Celebrate wins** – Recognize and reward progress along the way.

ABOUT THE AUTHOR

$\blacklozenge$

Ahmed Yahya is a seasoned business leader, strategist, and sales leadership expert with more than four decades of corporate and entrepreneurial experience. He began his career with General Motors as a Sales Analyst, quickly advancing to Sales Trainer, where he equipped sales teams across Saudi Arabia with the skills to excel. Over the next decade, he gained hands-on experience in every facet of sales operations, from field execution to strategic planning.

Ahmed later took on the challenge of joining an ambitious automotive dealership startup, where he first served as Sales and Marketing Director, moved on to Operations Director, before being appointed Managing Director. In these roles, he oversaw and drove the growth of the entire dealership operation, from sales and service to marketing, finance, and customer experience. Under his leadership, the organization scaled rapidly, sold thousands of vehicles in record time, and became one of Saudi Arabia's top-performing automotive retailers.

Drawing on a career spent at the helm of billion-dollar operations, Ahmed now shares his expertise through writing, speaking, and consulting, helping sales leaders master the strategies, trust, and team performance needed to achieve exceptional results.

REFERENCES

Adobe Experience Cloud Team. (2018, July 15). Is your lead really sales qualified? Here is how to tell. Adobe Experience Cloud. https://business.adobe.com/blog/basics/is-your-lead-sales-qualified-how-to-tell

Agbede, T. (2024, January 10). AI in sales: The trend & 7 ways to empower sales teams. Notta AI. https://www.notta.ai/en/blog/ai-for-sales

Alton, L. (2017, May 11). Phone calls, texts, or email. Here is how millennials prefer to communicate. Forbes. https://www.forbes.com/sites/larryalton/2017/05/11/how-do-millennials-prefer-to-communicate/

Baker, K. (2021). The ultimate guide to social media marketing campaigns. HubSpot. https://blog.hubspot.com/marketing/social-media-campaigns

Baker, K. (2023, June 7). The ultimate guide to content marketing in 2020. HubSpot. https://blog.hubspot.com/marketing/content-marketing

Bangia, M., Cruz, G., Huber, I., Landauer, P., & Sunku, V. (2020, May 13). Sales automation: The key to boosting revenue and reducing costs. McKinsey. https://www.mckinsey.com/capabilities/growth-marketing-and-sales/our-insights/sales-automation-the-key-to-boosting-revenue-and-reducing-costs

Baumgartner, T., Hatami, H., & Valdivieso, M. (2016, June 10). Why salespeople need to develop "machine intelligence." Harvard Business Review.

https://hbr.org/2016/06/why-salespeople-need-to-develop-machine-intelligence

Beheshti, N. (2019, January 16). 10 timely statistics about the connection between employee engagement and wellness. Forbes. https://www.forbes.com/sites/nazbeheshti/2019/01/16/10-timely-statistics-about-the-connection-between-employee-engagement-and-wellness/?sh=591a623822a0

Birt, J. (2023, September 29). What is a webinar and how does it work? (With tips). Indeed. https://www.indeed.com/career-advice/career-development/what-is-webinar

Bishop, C. (2024, February 2). Customer onboarding guide for 2023 (+6 best practices and examples). Zendesk. https://www.zendesk.com/blog/customer-onboarding/#:~:text=of%20customer%20onboarding-

Bray, M. (2023, October 25). Complete stakeholder mapping guide. MiroBlog. https://miro.com/blog/stakeholder-mapping/

Broadley, C. (2024, February 6). 25 lead generation form examples (That convert like crazy). WP Forms. https://wpforms.com/lead-generation-forms-examples/#:~:text=Asking%20yourself%20what%20is%20a

Brudner, E. (2022, September 14). 12 best sales methodologies & customer-centric selling systems. HubSpot. https://blog.hubspot.com/sales/6-popular-sales-methodologies-summarized

Chatterjee, S., Chaudhuri, R., & Vrontis, D. (2022). Big data analytics in strategic sales performance: mediating role of CRM capability and moderating role of leadership support. EuroMed Journal of Business. https://doi.org/10.1108/emjb-07-2021-0105

Ciotti, G. (2023, April 26). The business case for loving customers. Help Scout. https://www.helpscout.com/whole-company-support/

Coleman, B. (2023, June 9). How to create a sales territory plan: 5 simple steps. HubSpot. https://blog.hubspot.com/sales/how-to-strategically-divide-your-sales-territories

Coleman, B. (2024, January 31). How to write a great value proposition [7 top examples + template]. HubSpot. https://blog.hubspot.com/marketing/write-value-proposition

Cuncic, A. (2024, February 12). 7 active listening techniques for better communication. Verywell Mind. https://www.verywellmind.com/what-is-active-listening-3024343

Davies, C. (2022, September 2). The ultimate guide to sales prospecting: Tips, techniques, & tools to succeed. HubSpot. https://blog.hubspot.com/sales/prospecting

DealHub Experts. (2024, February 8). Sales funnel management. DealHub. https://dealhub.io/glossary/sales-funnel-management/

Evolution of sales management. (2022, December 5). The Intact One. https://theintactone.com/2022/12/05/evolution-of-sales-management/

Frost, A. (2021, July 26). SPIN selling: The ultimate guide. HubSpot. https://blog.hubspot.com/sales/spin-selling-the-ultimate-guide

Fuchs, J. (2022, August 30). How to understand &

thrive in digital sales. HubSpot.
https://blog.hubspot.com/sales/digital-sales

Gallo, A. (2014, June 23). How to help an
underperformer. Harvard Business Review.
https://hbr.org/2014/06/how-to-help-an-underperformer

Gangoli, A. (2022, October 20). Account mapping 101:
The complete guide to sales account mapping. DemandFarm.
https://www.demandfarm.com/blog/account-mapping-
101/#:~:text=The%20process%20of%20representing%20c
ustomer

Gargaro, D. (2023, November 15). Complete guide to
building a sales process. Business.
https://www.business.com/articles/sales-process/

Hargrave, M. (2023, July 31). What is CRM? Customer
relationship management defined. Investopedia.
https://www.investopedia.com/terms/c/customer_relation_m
anagement.asp#toc-types-of-crm

Hashemi-Pour, C. (2020). CRM (Customer relationship
management). TechTarget.
https://www.techtarget.com/searchcustomerexperience/defini
tion/CRM-customer-relationship-management

Hiltbrand, T. (2023, August 15). Empowering sales
through technology: How CIOs can drive sales success.
LinkedIn. https://www.linkedin.com/pulse/empowering-
sales-through-technology-how-cios-can-drive-troy-hiltbrand/

How big data analytics helps businesses increase their
revenue? (2023, May 29). LinkedIn.
https://www.linkedin.com/pulse/how-big-data-analytics-
helps-businesses-increase-revenue-matellio/

How do you plan and manage sales resources? (2023,

September 12). LinkedIn.
https://www.linkedin.com/advice/3/how-do-you-plan-
manage-sales-resources-skills-sales-
management#:~:text=You%20should%20consider%20fact
ors%20such

HubSpot. (n.d.). Customer feedback strategy: The only
guide you'll ever need. HubSpot.
https://www.hubspot.com/customer-feedback

Importance of a sales manager. (2012, August 30). Sales
Manager Now.
https://salesmanagernow.com/articles/importance-of-a-sales-
manager/

Indeed Editorial Team. (2022, June 25). 15 tips for
conducting your first sales performance review. Indeed.
https://www.indeed.com/career-advice/career-
development/sales-performance-review

Indeed Editorial Team. (2023a, February 4). KPI report:
How to share key performance data in 6 steps. Indeed.
https://www.indeed.com/career-advice/career-
development/how-to-report-kpis

Indeed Editorial Team. (2023b, February 4). 7 qualities
of an effective sales leader. Indeed.
https://www.indeed.com/career-advice/finding-a-job/sales-
leader

Indeed Editorial Team. (2023c, February 4). What is an
empathetic leader? (Definition, benefits and tips to become
one). Indeed. https://www.indeed.com/career-advice/career-
development/empathetic-leaders

Indeed Editorial Team. (2023d, March 11). Target
market analysis: What it is and how to make one. Indeed.
https://www.indeed.com/career-advice/career-

development/target-market-analysis

Indeed Editorial Team. (2023e, March 16). How to optimize the sales process (with tips and benefits). Indeed. https://www.indeed.com/career-advice/career-development/optimize-sales-process#:~:text=Optimizing%20your%20sales%20process%20means,improve%20your%20sales%20team%20strategies.

Indeed Editorial Team. (2023f, March 27). What is a price quote and what makes them important? Indeed. https://uk.indeed.com/career-advice/career-development/what-is-a-price-quote

Indeed Editorial Team. (2023g, August 1). Understanding constructive criticism: Definition, tips and examples. Indeed. https://www.indeed.com/career-advice/career-development/constructive-criticism

Jangra, A. (2023, December 30). ACAF customer feedback loop: Comprehensive guide. SupaHub. https://supahub.com/blog/acaf-customer-feedback-loop

Kelwig, D. (2022, July 12). Solution selling definition and techniques: The complete guide. Zendesk. https://www.zendesk.com/blog/solution-selling/

Kelwig, D. (2024, January 24). What is a sales CRM? Zendesk. https://www.zendesk.com/blog/sales-crm/

Kenton, W. (2023, October 30). SWOT analysis: How to with table and example. Investopedia. https://www.investopedia.com/terms/s/swot.asp

Kumar, A. (2022, September 12). What are the roles and responsibilities of a sales manager. Emeritus India. https://emeritus.org/in/learn/roles-and-responsibilities-of-a-sales-manager/

Leonard, K., & Watts, R. (2022, May 4). The ultimate guide to S.M.A.R.T. goals. Forbes. https://www.forbes.com/advisor/business/smart-goals/

limaye, S., & Pande, Dr. M. (2016). Are there ethics in sales profession – A study. International Journal of Scientific Research and Management, 04(03). https://doi.org/10.18535/ijsrm/v4i3.06

Lucid Content Team. (2019, December 16). All about the N.E.A.T. Selling™ methodology. Lucidchart. https://www.lucidchart.com/blog/neat-selling-explained

Mares, J. (2023, June 13). A 5-minute summary of "the challenger sale" book your boss told you to read. HubSpot. https://blog.hubspot.com/sales/challenger-sale-summary

Marr, B. (2022, August 5). 13 easy steps to improve your critical thinking skills. Forbes. https://www.forbes.com/sites/bernardmarr/2022/08/05/13-easy-steps-to-improve-your-critical-thinking-skills/?sh=7feb4e025ecd

Martin, S. (2011, June 27). Seven personality traits of top salespeople. Harvard Business Review. https://hbr.org/2011/06/the-seven-personality-traits-o

McGlauflin, P., & Abrams, J. (2023, September 21). Employees who receive unactionable performance feedback are more likely to quit. Fortune. https://fortune.com/2023/09/21/women-feedback-performance-review-bias-quit/

Nash, B. (2023, August 20). What is SNAP selling? GTMnow. https://gtmnow.com/snap-selling/

Needle, F. (2023, December 5). How to create detailed

buyer personas for your business [+free persona template]. HubSpot. https://blog.hubspot.com/marketing/buyer-persona-research

O'Bryan, A. (2022, February 8). How to practice active listening: 16 examples & techniques. PositivePsychology.com. https://positivepsychology.com/active-listening-techniques/

102 sales motivational quotes to inspire your sales team. (n.d.). Pipedrive. https://www.pipedrive.com/en/blog/motivational-sales-quotes

Redbord, M. (2023, August 2). The hard truth about acquisition costs (and how your customers can save you). HubSpot. https://blog.hubspot.com/service/customer-acquisition-study?hubs_content=www.hubspot.com%2Fcustomer-feedback&hubs_content-cta=93%25%20of%20customers&_gl=1

Roberts, D. (2023, July 1). Curiosity is one of the most valuable traits you can employ as a leader. Inc. https://www.inc.com/debra-roberts/curiosity-is-one-of-most-valuable-traits-you-can-employ-as-a-leader.html

Robertson, C. (2020, June 23). What are the sustained implications of COVID-19? Here's what our B2B marketing and sales analysts see. Forrester. https://www.forrester.com/blogs/what-are-the-sustained-implications-of-covid-19-heres-what-our-b2b-marketing-and-sales-analysts-see/

7 reasons why honesty is an effective sales strategy. (2019, September 12). Cydcor. https://www.cydcor.com/7-reasons-why-honesty-is-the-most-effective-sales-strategy/

Shewan, D. (2023, October 30). 7 of the best value proposition examples we've ever seen. WordStream. https://www.wordstream.com/blog/ws/2016/04/27/value-proposition-examples

60 motivational sales quotes to fire up your sales representatives. (2020, March 26). VerbTEAMS. https://solofire.com/blog/60-motivational-sales-quotes-to-fire-up-your-sales-representatives/

Success story business manager Philip Meijer. (n.d.). Vibe Group. https://vibegroup.com/careers/en/blog/philips-success-story-from-salesman-to-business-manager-in-six-years/

SugarCRM. (2023, December 14). The future of CRM software: 4 trends sales leaders will be seeing in 2024 and beyond. LinkedIn. https://www.linkedin.com/pulse/future-crm-software-4-trends-sales-leaders-seeing-2024-beyond-zzl7f/

Talbot, P. (2021, July 13). The shifting landscape of brand loyalty. Forbes. https://www.forbes.com/sites/paultalbot/2021/07/13/the-shifting-landscape-of-brand-loyalty/?sh=5147435a3d14

Taylor, B. (2023, March 29). Consultative selling: 7 ways to sell based on need. HubSpot. https://blog.hubspot.com/sales/consultative-selling

Trent, C. (2022, February 7). 15 shocking sales follow-up statistics that will light a fire under you (2022). Dooly. https://www.dooly.ai/blog/sales-follow-up-statistics/

Turkington, A. (2023, May 4). How to close a sale: 7 closing techniques & why they work. HubSpot. https://blog.hubspot.com/sales/sales-closing-techniques-and-why-they-work

Twin, A. (2024, January 30). Understanding key performance indicators (KPIs). Investopedia. https://www.investopedia.com/terms/k/kpi.asp#:~:text=Key%20performance%20indicators%20(KPIs)%20measure

Tyre, D. (2023, October 6). What is a sales funnel? (& what you should make instead). Hubspot. https://blog.hubspot.com/sales/sales-funnel

Van Rensburg, I. (2022, October 10). How to create an ideal customer profile (ICP) with template. Cognism. https://www.cognism.com/blog/ideal-customer-profile#:~:text=An%20ideal%20customer%20profile%20(ICP)%20is%20a%20description%20of%20the

Victorino, R. (2020, September 23). The Eisenhower matrix: Prioritize your time on what matters most - Knock down silos. Slab. https://slab.com/blog/eisenhower-matrix/

Weaver, A. (2023, June 9). Sales process fundamentals: A guide to consistently closing deals in a changing world. Zendesk UK. https://www.zendesk.co.uk/blog/sales-process/

Wilkinson, I. (2023, July 21). How to build long term relationships with customers. Spiralytics. https://www.spiralytics.com/blog/7-successful-ways-to-establish-long-term-relationships-with-your-clients/

Ye, L. (2022, December 7). Objection handling: 44 common sales objections & how to respond. HubSpot. https://blog.hubspot.com/sales/handling-common-sales-objections

www.ingramcontent.com/pod-product-compliance
Lightning Source LLC
Chambersburg PA
CBHW071707210326
41597CB00017B/2371